Teaching
READING to
ENGLISH
LANGUAGE LEARNERS,
Grades 6–12

Teaching READING to ENGLISH LANGUAGE LEARNERS,

Grades 6–12

A Framework
for Improving
Achievement in
the Content Areas

MARGARITA
CALDERÓN

CORWIN PRESS
A SAGE Publications Company
Thousand Oaks, CA 91320

For information:

Corwin Press
A Sage Publications Company
2455 Teller Road
Thousand Oaks, California 91320
www.corwinpress.com

Sage Publications India Pvt. Ltd.
B 1/I 1 Mohan Cooperative
  Industrial Area
Mathura Road, New Delhi 110 044
India

Sage Publications Ltd.
1 Oliver's Yard
55 City Road
London EC1Y 1SP
United Kingdom

Sage Publications Asia-Pacific Pte. Ltd.
33 Pekin Street #02-01
Far East Square
Singapore 048763

Printed in the United States of America.

Library of Congress Cataloging-in-Publication Data

Calderón, Margarita.
Teaching reading to English language learners, grades 6–12: A framework for improving achievement in the content areas / Margarita Calderón.
    p. cm.
Includes bibliographical references and index.
ISBN 978-1-4129-0925-9 (cloth)
ISBN 978-1-4129-0926-6 (pbk.)
1. English language—Study and teaching (Middle school)—Foreign speakers.
2. English language—Study and teaching (Secondary)—Foreign speakers.
3. Content area reading. I. Title.

PE1128.A2C25 2007
428.2′4 —dc22   2006034138

This book is printed on acid-free paper.

07 08 09 10 11 10 9 8 7 6 5 4 3 2 1

Acquisitions Editor:	Rachel Livsey
Editorial Assistant:	Phyllis Cappello
Production Editor:	Diane S. Foster
Copy Editor:	Gretchen A. Treadwell and Theresa Kay
Typesetter:	C&M Digitals (P) Ltd.
Proofreader:	Caryne Brown
Indexer:	Molly Hall
Cover Designer:	Monique Hahn
Graphic Designer:	Scott Van Atta

Contents

Preface

Secondary ELL students are more likely to have experienced such challenges as interrupted schooling and zero-English proficiency, which require substantial educational growth in a short amount of time. Secondary-school-age children present educators with unique and specific challenges for instruction and language acquisition.

This book attempts to address some of these challenges by combining research and practice as it emerges from a set of longitudinal studies in various parts of the United States and other English-speaking territories/countries. The Carnegie Corporation of New York, the U.S. Department of Education's Institute for Education Sciences, and the U.S. Department of Education's Native Americans Projects have funded these studies. Standardized language and reading and subject-matter measures, as well as formative assessments, are being used to collect information on what strategies are successful in closing the achievement gap for English learners from different language backgrounds, learning in a variety of English immersion, sheltered English, and dual language programs.

Developing literacy skills for secondary school students is not easy. Secondary school literacy skills are more complex and more embedded in subject matters than in primary schools (Biancarosa & Snow, 2004). In their recent publication on adolescent literacy entitled *Reading Next*, these two authors assert that subject matter literacy

- Includes reading, writing, and oral discourse for school
- Varies from subject to subject
- Requires knowledge of multiple genres of text, purposes for text use, and text media
- Is influenced by students' literacies in contexts outside of school
- Is influenced by students' personal, social, and cultural experiences

For English language learners and struggling older readers, reading becomes an insurmountable task without explicit instruction on reading each of the subject matter texts. Fortunately, through ongoing studies specifically designed for adolescent ELL literacy, educators now have a powerful array of tools at their disposal. We even know from the data that these tools work well for non-ELL struggling readers. We have spent 3 years "components testing" to find the best instructional and professional development combinations for addressing students' and teachers' needs. The combination of components, strategies, and performance assessment tools has been arranged in a framework that we call Expediting Comprehension for English Language Learners (ExC-ELL).

Recommendations for Instructional Components

We have identified 12 components for this framework. Some components are aimed at helping teachers improve student achievement. Others are for helping teachers be successful themselves. These are the recommendations derived from the multiple ongoing studies thus far:

1. Teachers need assistance and models for developing lessons that integrate subject matter content, language, reading, and writing skills. The first five components help teachers integrate these features into a cohesive lesson plan.

2. Teaching subject matter to ELLs requires direct, explicit instruction in the strategies students need to build vocabulary and comprehend grade-level texts.

3. Students need to learn how to read a variety of texts that progress to grade-level texts quickly. In order to master content and meet standards, teachers learn how to parse texts and select most important content. Teachers select the district's content standards, objective, indicators ("I can" statements), purposes, outcomes, and targets, and scan the text once more for eliminating unnecessary information and highlighting information that addresses the standard.

4. Explicitly teaching depth and breadth of words before, during, and after reading is a primary role of all content teachers.

5. Collaborative-text-based reading engages students with text and rich discussions where the new words are used again and again.

6. Explicitly teaching reading and writing skills is just as important in secondary as it is in elementary schools, notwithstanding adaptations in delivery:

   - Teachers select comprehension strategy (e.g., main idea, cause and effect, inferences, comparing/contrasting, self-correction, rereading a sentence, decoding a word, summarizing, questioning the author, questioning the information in the text, questioning ourselves.
   - Teachers conduct read-alouds to model fluency and comprehension strategies.
   - Students conduct partner reading to practice comprehension strategies and comprehend content.
   - Teachers debrief with whole class about the content and the skills (linguistic, metalinguistic, comprehension, social, and cooperative learning) that they learned.

7. Explicitly teaching the different writing genre required by each content area, including the various formats for technology.

8. Consolidation of content and skills. Teachers use strategies throughout the lesson to anchor knowledge, check for understanding, and assess individual student learning.

9. Student assessments include a variety of formats to gauge progress on literacy and content.

10. The quality of implementation is assessed with specific observation protocols supported by technology in order to have instant reports for teachers and administrators. Coaches and administrators need to be trained to observe this type of instruction.

11. Systematic and comprehensive professional development throughout the year is necessary to sustain any program, approach, or instructional change.

12. Teachers Learning Communities for collegial work help teachers with implementation hurdles and to learn from one another.

Overall Organization of the Book

Since using only 3 or 4 of these components is unlikely to yield positive results for students or teachers, the chapters include lesson designs that consolidate all components.

Chapter 1. The introductory chapter details the background of the ExC-ELL study. It also states several "myths" that have been around for many years, such as "it takes 7 years to learn a language," which often hold back students and keep teachers from delivering challenging, rigorous, yet sensitive instruction to ELLs. Each myth is followed by a "good news" section that dispels that myth and offers empirically tested recommendations instead.

Chapter 2. This chapter gives a detailed background of the research for each of the ExC-ELL components. Each component was carefully selected based on the amount of reliable scientific research available. Each of the 10 lesson components was empirically tested across a variety of classrooms and with different language groups to gauge applicability and appropriateness. Refinements were made during the first two years of the study.

Chapter 3. This chapter goes further in depth about vocabulary. The theoretical framework for selecting and teaching vocabulary to ELLs was presented at the Pacific Regional Educational Laboratory conference on Vocabulary: Research and Practice, where researchers such as Isabel Beck, Diane August, Freddie Hiebert, Michael Kamil, Steve Stahl, and others were kind enough to give me feedback. Once refined, we tested a few instructional strategies and then let the teachers run free with their own creative ways of teaching. In the ExC-ELL lesson delivery sequence, the teacher begins with vocabulary instruction so students can comprehend and interact during background building of concepts, reading, processing and mastering information, and writing activities. The strategies shared in Chapter 3 are some that teachers felt were most successful.

Chapter 4. This chapter deals with the heart of the program—reading comprehension. While it presents comprehension strategies that work with ELLs, it also emphasizes all the other instructional features that need to be in place for comprehension to work. It presents ideas for consolidating student knowledge after they have read a text. The consolidation of knowledge can take several forms, from instructional conversations with the teacher to graphic organizers in teams to writing activities, and finally debriefing with students what they have learned. There needs to be a different approach to teaching reading in secondary schools. Therefore, a set of guiding questions is used to help teachers integrate reading into their existing lessons and content standards.

Chapter 5. This chapter provides the rationale for teaching math vocabulary in the way proposed. It also lays out a lesson design for integrating vocabulary and reading skills development. Student-centered activities through Cooperative Learning are suggested for further practice of concepts and language.

Chapters 6, 7, and 8. These chapters are similar to the math chapter, but Chapter 6 uses science, and Chapter 7 uses language arts to provide examples of integrated lessons. Since each content area is approached differently through textbooks or its particular textual genre, the lessons vary in some aspects.

Chapter 9. This chapter steers away from curriculum and lesson design to a critical topic: professional development and continuous learning communities in schools. After a summer institute on programs such as ExC-ELL, school administrators want to know what is the best follow-up and systematic support they can give to their teachers so all new learnings are implemented with quality and as much comfort as possible for the teacher. This chapter offers ideas on sustaining the innovation through various support mechanisms.

Chapter 10. This chapter provides tools for literacy coaches, content coaches, and supervisors on how to observe, reflect, and coach teachers implementing ExC-ELL using the ExC-ELL Observation Protocol. The Protocol can also be used by the teachers to observe their students, to plan their lessons, and to reflect on their practice.

Acknowledgments

I would like to begin by thanking Dr. Liliana Minaya-Rowe for her collaboration on the ExC-ELL project from its inception, and acknowledge her contributions to this manual with the social studies lesson ethnography, graphic organizers and references.

I also want to thank Argelia Carreón, who contributed conceptually to the reading comprehension component. Both Liliana and Argelia have been terrific trainers of teachers and fantastic friends.

I want to particularly thank Andrés Henríquez at the Carnegie Corporation of New York for his ideas, support, and the trust he placed in us as we plunged into unknown waters. The editing by Ashley Fitch and María Trejo helped tremendously. Finally, Diane August and the following teachers and administrators contributed to the development of the instructional strategies and professional development model in Phase 1 of the study:

Kapa'a Middle School:

Roberta Zarbaugh
Jim Cox
Fig Mitchell
Terry Maguire
Rene Relación
Debra Gochros

Kapa'a High School:

Margaret Clapp
Kara Panui
Wendy Schwarze
Janis Gowan
Todd Barcial
Edwin Phillips
Susan Sobel

Kauai District Office

Daniel Hamada, Complex Area Superintendent

Naomi Nishida, Curriculum Educational Specialist

Ligaya Ortal, ESL Resource Teacher

Sandra Haynes, Literacy Resource Teacher

April Shigemoto, Assessment Liaison Resource Teacher

Gilmore Youn, Kapa'a High School Principal

Mary Ann Bode, Kapa'a Middle School Principal

Jason Kuloloia, Kapa'a Middle School Interim Principal

Pilot teachers and administrators from Guillen Middle School and Bowie High School of the El Paso Independent School District and West Middle School in Waterbury, Connecticut.

The contributions of the following reviewers are gratefully acknowledged:

Mary Enright
National Board Certified Teacher
New York State Education Department
Office of Bilingual Education
Albany, NY

Al Payne
Administrative Director
Regional Center IV
Miami-Dade County Public Schools
Miami, FL

Patricia Schwartz
Principal
Thomas Jefferson Middle School
Teaneck, NJ

Neal Glasgow
Teacher and Author
San Dieguito Academy
Encinitas, CA

Arlene Myslinski
ELL Teacher
Buffalo Grove High School
Buffalo Grove, IL

David Bautista
Bilingual Director
Woodburn School District
Western University
Woodburn, OR

Nadia Mykysey
Adjunct Faculty at Temple University
Curriculum, Instruction and Technology in Education (CITE)
Philadelphia, PA

About the Author

 **Margarita Calderón,** a native of Juárez, Mexico, is a senior research scientist and professor at Johns Hopkins University's School of Professional Studies in Business and Education.

She is serving on several national panels: the National Research Council's Committee on Teacher Preparation; the U. S. Department of Education Institute for Education Sciences' National Literacy Panel for Language Minority Children and Youth; the Carnegie Adolescent English Language Learners Literacy Panel; and the California Pre-School Biliteracy Panel.

She is principal investigator in three five-year studies on *Expediting Reading Comprehension for English Language Learners (ExCELL) Programs,* one that focuses on professional development of science, social studies, and language arts teachers in New York City's middle and high schools, funded by the Carnegie Corporation of New York; and two other studies funded by the U. S. Department of Education in the Pacific Islands for fourth- and fifth-grade teachers and students, and in middle and high schools in Alaska.

She is coprincipal investigator with Robert Slavin on the five-year national randomized evaluation of English immersion, transitional, and two-way bilingual programs, funded by the Institute for Education Sciences

She has published over 100 articles, chapters, books, and teacher training manuals.

To my brilliant Luis Mauricio.
To my marvelous associates Lupe, María, Liliana,
Argelia, Lili, Daniel, Rubén, and Rebecca.

1

Introduction

The ExC-ELL Model—Literacy and English Language Learners

"How can my ELLs ever catch up?"

—tenth-grade government teacher

Many middle and high school teachers and principals are asking us what to do about the large numbers of English language learners (ELLs) coming to their schools. The way they have been teaching English as a Second Language is not working. Trying to address all the newcomers and the variety of proficiency levels of ELLs across the grade levels overwhelms the lone ranger ESL teacher. Teachers can't find enough sheltered materials that cover the important facts and concepts, much less the district's standards. The seventh- and tenth-grade ELLs are not passing the high-stakes tests. Teachers and principals are being held accountable for poor test scores, and both fear their jobs are on the line.

Organizations such as the Alliance for Excellent Education (www .a114ed.org), National Association of Secondary School Principals (www.nassp.org), and the Carnegie Corporation of New York (www .carnegie.org) have also been preoccupied with this issue. The Carnegie Corporation approached us in 2002 to develop a professional development program that could begin to address the needs of ELLs and teachers in secondary schools.

Thus, the Project *Expediting Comprehension for English Language Learners (ExC-ELL®)* was funded in 2003 by the Carnegie Corporation of New York to develop and study the effects of a professional development model for *middle and high school teachers of English, science, mathematics, and social studies who work with ELLs.*

The purpose of this book is to share the professional development and instructional components developed and tested in sixth- to twelfth-grade classrooms. The information and strategies outlined in subsequent chapters were tested from Connecticut to Hawaii in classrooms with multiple language student backgrounds.

Why the Program Worked

Since most ELLs are in heterogeneous classrooms that include English-only students (in the five pilot schools, the number ranged from 10% to 90% ELLs in each classroom), the staff development program was designed to help teachers provide effective instruction *for ELLs and all other students in their classrooms, particularly those reading below grade level and needing extensive vocabulary development.* Student data indicated significant results not just for ELLs but also for all students in the participating classrooms. Teachers reported these same strategies were particularly helpful with African American and Hawaiian students who needed additional work with vocabulary and reading skills. The professional development and instructional components are described in chapters throughout this book.

In addition to the teacher training program, professional development sessions were designed for *literacy coaches, content curriculum specialists, principals, and central office administrators* on how to observe and coach teachers as they deliver their lessons integrating reading, writing, and vocabulary development along with their content. The ExC-ELL Observation Protocol (EOP) was developed and tested for validity and reliability by teams consisting of a principal, associate superintendent, coach, university professor, and teacher.

The ExC-ELL Observation Protocol® was used as a classroom tool for

- Planning content lessons
- Coaching by literacy coaches not familiar with ELL instruction
- Supervision by administrators
- Teacher self-reflection
- Peer coaching
- Conducting classroom research

After the exciting results from the first study, the Carnegie Corporation provided funding for a second phase of ExC-ELL to test the feasibility of the observation protocol with handheld technology. This is being done in conjunction with Wireless Generation, which developed the software and worked closely with Johns Hopkins to design a computer-based version of the protocol. The project is being implemented in New York City schools and studied for the next two years.

A second five-year study will be training teachers of different Alaskan Native American students. All these ongoing studies will help to fine tune ExC-ELL and share results continuously.

Benefits for Schools, Principals, Teachers, and Students

No Child Left Behind calls for reform and accountability for all English language learners (ELLs) and all students reading below grade level. In particular, secondary schools need to improve and need help toward that goal. If schools want to improve student performance it means they must begin by improving the performance of all teachers, particularly teachers in middle and high schools who have *ELLs and other adolescents reading below grade level.*

The limited English language skills and low academic performance of Hispanic and other language-minority students pose a major problem in the middle and high school settings. Middle school and high school language-minority students must be ready to participate in a rigorous academic program, and the time for this preparation is limited, which often allows ELLs only superficial learning of vocabulary and concepts. Thus, they are never up to par with the literacy levels and academics demanded by secondary school curricula.

Consequently, most middle and high school language-minority students fail to develop to their fullest potential. As a result, they become disaffected, drop out of school, have to settle for low-paying jobs or no job at all because they have little or no access to either high school or a college education (RAND, 2001; Slavin & Calderón, 2001).

Most teachers do not receive preparation to teach the language-minority students before entering the workforce and have limited opportunities to update their knowledge and skills in an ongoing basis throughout their careers (Calderón & Minaya-Rowe, 2003). The teachers' lack of preparedness is a serious problem because the opportunities for at-risk students to succeed academically depend on teachers' knowledge and application of effective teaching in the classroom (National Education Association, 2003). According to the U.S. Department of Education, 42% of public school teachers have at least one ELL in the classroom, only 27% of teachers of ELLs feel highly qualified to teach them, and only 30% of teachers of ELLs have received professional development in teaching these students (Leos, 2005). The Learning First Alliance (2000) reports teachers in general may be educated, licensed, and employed without knowledge of the most important tools for fighting illiteracy.

To equip all teachers to work successfully with a growing at-risk population requires continuing renewal and extension of the skills, knowledge, and awareness needed to remain effective in a multicultural dynamic environment (Darling-Hammond & Sykes, 1999). NCLB calls for professional qualifications of teachers and profound knowledge of, among other topics,

- Student academic achievement disaggregated by subgroups;
- Comparison of students at basic, proficient, and advanced levels of language and literacy development;
- Assessment processes, interpretation of data, implications for instructional improvement;
- An ample instructional repertoire that reaches all students.

> Teachers cannot possibly be fully prepared without quality preservice and quality ongoing professional development. Results-driven education and quality teaching require teacher-focused quality professional development.

New and experienced teachers need the type of professional development that allows them to explore their beliefs about their students and increase their repertoire of linguistic and culturally relevant pedagogy (Calderón,

2000). This also places teachers' needs within a larger context that includes institutional mission and goals, student performance data, and teacher support mechanisms. An institution's program (school district or university) must include measures for student performance and for measuring changes in educators' on-the-job performance. But it must also apply those same measures to the institution preparing the teachers.

One area that needs dire attention and quality comprehensive professional development programs is *reading*. Although everyone in the nation is preoccupied with developing reading skills for all students, including ELLs, scarce attention is given to effective designs of professional programs to develop the teachers' skills for *teaching reading within the context of rigorous content instruction*.

Myths From the Past That Still Haunt Us!—But There's Good News!

Although there is quite an emerging interest in ELLs at secondary schools (*Reading Next* Report; Department of Education's focus on adolescent literacy), there have been prevalent beliefs, practices, and policies that have prevented the implementation of quality instructional programs for ELLs. Some misconceptions have been:

- The belief that it takes 5 to 7 years to become proficient in English.
- The misconception that ESL or sheltered instruction teachers can meet all the needs of each ELL student by themselves, and mainstream content teachers do not have to and cannot teach ELLs.
- The focus of instruction in English as a second language (ESL) classrooms should be oral language development.
- Special classes need to be set up where content and English are simplified to the point that they are watered down in order to make them comprehensible for ELLs.
- All ELLs need the same type of ESL program, same phonics-based interventions, and to be placed in the same classroom together.

YES, *it used to* take five to seven years. It may still take that long when ELLs are placed in elementary schools where the transition from primary language into

> **MYTH:** It takes five to seven years to become proficient in English.

English instruction is delayed until the fourth, fifth, or sixth grades. By then, it is too late for students to catch up and be fully prepared for middle school. It may also take five to seven years when the pacing of instruction is too relaxed and not challenging enough. After spending five to seven years learning only or mainly in their primary language, students become accustomed and do not feel the need to learn English, since they've gotten along without it for so long. As they go up the grade levels, the difficulty of the dense textbooks they encounter also goes up. This becomes a greater and greater challenge when students are not used to rigorous (but relevant and sensitive) instruction in English.

At the other extreme, instruction in the early grades might have been paced so fast students could never catch up! This fast-track pacing leaves huge gaps in the normal development of basic skills such as grammar, spelling, composition, and most important, reading comprehension. If these students are then transitioned into all-English instruction in the first or second grade, they may never catch up.

In secondary schools, Newcomers, Students with Interrupted Formal Education (SIFE), or even lifelong ELLs are clustered together. Either they are immersed in content classes immediately into difficult content courses with pull-out or push-in ESL support (which has no evidence of being effective), or they take ESL and sheltered content classes that may not be rigorous enough to catch up to standards. The extreme practices in schools imply the *balancing act between rigor, relevancy, and sensitivity* is what we want all teachers of ELLs to achieve in their active teaching repertoires.

Good News: Through several randomized scientific studies, we are seeing how instruction can be carefully crafted to accelerate the learning rate of literacy in English at whatever grade level ELLs enter. These studies also show instruction can facilitate the learning of two languages simultaneously. For instance, students can learn to speak, read, and write in English and Spanish in two-way bilingual programs (TWB). In two-way/dual-language bilingual programs, mainstream and language minority students become bilingual and biliterate when instructed in both languages from prekindergarten on—just as many people in other countries have done for centuries. Well-designed dual-language programs for middle and high schools are now functioning effectively in sites such as El Paso, Texas and New York City.

MYTH: ESL or sheltered instruction teachers can meet all the needs of each ELL student by themselves and mainstream content teachers do not have to and cannot teach ELLs.

The NCLB testing requirements for secondary schools are having detrimental effects on ELLs. The Hispanic dropout rate is at its highest in history. English language learners are not meeting AYP. Those students who make it to universities face a 75% chance they will fail and drop out the first year. If school administrators want their ELLs to show annual yearly progress, to pass state assessments, and to succeed in life, then they must hire well-prepared teachers or prepare them through comprehensive inservice programs, with the latter being the most viable option.

Every state in the nation will attest to the fact that there is a critical shortage of bilingual and ESL credentialed teachers, particularly secondary teachers. However, this does not preclude offering professional development for teachers in the field who are working with a handful or majority numbers of ELLs in their classrooms. In fact, providing professional development should be a requirement. As a result, NCLB calls for highly qualified teachers in core subjects, and that should include Language Arts or English as a second language. Some states require all educators (teachers and administrators) to have some coursework on working with ELL populations, but teachers report it is rarely sufficient to address their students' needs, particularly when it comes to ELL reading difficulties.

Good News: Some schools, districts, and state departments of education have already taken steps toward and beyond NCLB requirements by offering comprehensive professional development programs for *all* their teachers. State departments of education, such as the one in Washington state, began training all educators on ELL issues in 2005. New York City schools began retraining hundreds of teachers on current research-based literacy in Spanish and updated methods for ESL. They went as far as offering schools $20,000 to begin planning ways of restructuring their programs to better address the needs of ELLs and to establish more two-way bilingual schools. The island of Kauai began setting the pace for other islands in the state of Hawaii. They accomplished this by establishing, at the district level, learning communities

> **MYTH:** The focus of instruction in the English as a second language (ESL) classroom should be oral language development.

where the superintendent and his education specialists worked collaboratively to learn and create ways of supporting learning for all educators in the district with a strong focus on ELL literacy.

In most secondary schools, there appears to be a chasm between the ESL and the content classrooms. The ESL teacher is supposed to concentrate on "getting those kids to speak English" and the content teachers to impart content. For decades, ESL meant learning basic words in English, enough to help students express themselves and understand basic instructions from teachers in mainstream classrooms. This very basic vocabulary is what we call Tier 1 words. They are important for building Tier 2 and 3 word knowledge germane to conceptual understanding of the sciences, social studies, and math coursework (for a broader definition and examples of Tier 1–3 words, please see Chapter 3). However, a whole semester or more is definitely too long in a student's scholastic life to spend on Tier 1 words. For example, we recently observed a high school ESL teacher who spent 50 minutes teaching 10 words about professions (e.g., carpenter, engineer, teacher). The teacher used props, pictures, and gestures to present each word. After providing information on each, he asked his eight students to work in pairs to match the words with a definition he provided in an envelope. He walked around and helped the students who needed help. The students mostly worked silently, moving the pieces around, until the teacher gave them a thumbs up. Before the period ended, we decided to give the students a test on the 10 words. The most they remembered were five words. In other words, 50 minutes were spent "teaching" but not "reaching." This instructional event reinforces how ESL teachers may be doing a lot of work, well intended, but not in the most efficient and effective manner.

Good News: In the past two years, research that focuses on vocabulary development for mainstream and ELLs has shown promising practices for accelerating the learning of vocabulary in both ESL and mainstream classrooms. Although it is important to teach oral language, it does not have to be separate from reading and writing development. In fact, exposure to the written word and basic reading skills helps students develop a larger vocabulary. Student mastery of a word means they can decode, pronounce, spell, define it, write a meaningful sentence with it, and recognize it in a different context. Ways of expediting mastery of words are described in the vocabulary chapter.

MYTH: Special classes need to be set up where content and English are sheltered in order to make them comprehensible for ELLs.

The term *sheltered classes* or *ESL content classes* are sometimes misconstrued as places where subject matter is adapted and/or watered down to very simplistic oral phrases and superficial concepts. Sheltered instruction calls for the teacher to use "appropriate speech" (Echevarria, Vogt, & Short, 2004), which at times turns out to be taught in a way that limits the growth of vocabulary. We observed a teacher who was so careful to select words her students would understand that she limited her vocabulary all semester long as well as the students' breadth and depth of word knowledge.

Students' linguistic and academic development is enormously hindered when they have to submit to semesters of this type of limited instruction. In cases like this, sheltered instruction focuses too much on making content comprehensible to an extreme. When it takes too much time for the teacher to show pictures, realia, make gestures, it leaves little time for students to interact with the new words and take ownership. Although sheltered classes are intended to make rigorous content comprehensible, ESL/sheltered content teachers need to monitor the extent of sheltering and the benefits students are deriving.

Good News: Academic language proficiency is the ability to make complex meanings explicit using appropriate language for that specific content area. It's not communicating through paralinguistic cues or choppy phrases. Academic language proficiency is the ability to read, discuss, and write about complex topics learned in school. All teachers—ESL, sheltered instruction, mainstream—can now be well equipped with ways to help students attain academic language proficiency.

English language learners come to secondary schools with a wide range of linguistic, academic, and life skills. Typically, schools offer only one type of ESL course per grade level, where the whole range of students are placed. This makes it very difficult for the ESL teacher to address the array of needs. This teacher will most likely try to teach to the middle, limiting quality attention and instruction to the students in the higher and lower ends of the continuum.

> **MYTH:** All ELLs need the same type of ESL program, same phonics-based interventions, and to be placed in the same classroom together.

The term **"differentiated instruction"** has come to mean a mainstream teacher can have a wide range of students in the same class and can use certain strategies to cope with this diversity. No matter how skilled a teacher is or how many inservices on differentiated instruction they have attended, they may not address literacy and oracy development.

In some cases many ELLs' problems stem not from lack of oral language development but from a diversity of reading development difficulties. They are able to express themselves in English quite well. These students may or may not be identified as Limited English Proficient (LEP) but have great difficulty comprehending texts in English. They have been poorly schooled and will need some basic phonics, along with phonemic and phonological awareness activities through immediate interventions or in the context of reading. However, studies indicate after 20 or so lessons on phonics only, the effect diminished considerably (Kamil, 2006). Therefore, *semester-long phonics programs/instruction without focusing on other skills will not work for ELLs.*

In contrast, other ELLs are so well schooled and literate they would feel insulted attending such phonics/phonemic awareness interventions. The intervention they need is ample vocabulary development and acquaintance with the basic protocols of classroom norms, social norms, an understanding of their teachers' expectations, and the variety of concepts of print for all the textbooks they will be using.

Good News: When schools are sensitive to their students, they find ways of assessing each student to find out what type of intervention is necessary—decoding, contrastive linguistics, fluency in speaking, fluency in reading, reading comprehension, spelling, writing mechanics, composition, more vocabulary development, grammar, etc. The amount of time for the intervention also varies. Some students may need a whole semester of reading instruction while others only one-on-one tutoring for two or three weeks. Expediting reading comprehension entails providing the right type of instructional intervention as expeditiously as possible. This means the reading specialists must be well trained to have an extensive repertoire of reading strategies and techniques. They must also have appropriate materials to cover the range of necessary interventions. The interventions can take place after school, on Saturdays, or as electives. It is important to begin interventions as soon as possible at the beginning of the semester and to end the intervention when it is no longer necessary.

Summary

- ✓ There are many prevalent myths about ELL instruction that keep teachers and students from reaching full potential.

- ✓ ELLs benefit from carefully crafted and challenging content instruction.

✓ Teaching reading comprehension in the content areas can be achieved by combining components that have been empirically tested in classrooms with ELLs.

✓ Successful teachers are supported by caring and knowledgeable coaches and administrators who also know how reading and content go together.

2

Planning Lessons Using a Research-Based Design

The literacy constructs described in Chapter 4 were incorporated into a 10-component instructional template that mainstream and ESL teachers piloted in a 2-year study through Project ExC-ELL funded by the Carnegie Corporation of New York. This last year, as these teachers continue to apply and develop new lessons, the 10 basic components remain. These lessons are being used in fourth- through twelfth-grade science, social studies, math, language arts, and ESL classes. The class periods that range from 45 minutes to 90 minutes in secondary schools. In some cases, it takes three days to complete a cycle, depending on the content and the reading selections. For the most part, teachers apply the 10 components in the sequence outlined in the box. *(Please see samples of lessons in the following chapters.)*

Lesson Template

1. Teachers select the district's content standard, objective, indicators ("I can" statements), purpose, outcomes and targets, and scan the text for information that addresses the standard.

2. Parsing of text by teachers. Teachers preview the expository or narrative text (textbook chapter, literature section, poem, etc.) to select, condense, and eliminate unnecessary information and segment the text for explicit instruction.

3. Summarization/overview of unit, lesson, chapter. Teacher writes a short summary for sharing with students before, during, or after the lesson introduction.

4. Background building of concepts. Teachers use graphics, films, pictures, real objects, or concepts of print (title, headings, charts, graphs) in the selected text to provide an anticipatory set of main concepts.

5. Review previous lesson/concepts/content. Teachers connect new information with previous information learned.

6. Vocabulary
   - Teachers select Tier 1, 2, and 3 words for background building, for pre-teaching, for teaching on the run as the teacher conducts a read aloud, and for follow-up activities with the new words after students have read the text.
   - Teachers select method/technique for teaching each word (e.g., ESL technique, Beck strategy, Parking Lot, semantic map, Roundtable, word bank).
   - Teachers write debriefing questions that focus on word knowledge and strategies for figuring out unfamiliar words.

7. Formulate questions for drawing background knowledge. Teachers write out questions to use before reading, during reading, and after reading to check for comprehension every step of the way.

8. Engagement with text.
   - Teachers select comprehension strategy (e.g., clarifying, finding main idea, cause and effect, making inferences, comparing/contrasting, self-correction, rereading a sentence, decoding a word, summarizing a couple of sentences, questioning the author/text, questioning ourselves).

- Teachers model the use of metalinguistic skills to figure out new words, and metacognitive skills to figure out how to learn content by using skills previously learned (e.g., in elementary school, in the primary language).
- Teachers conduct read-alouds to model fluency and comprehension strategies.
- Students conduct partner reading to practice comprehension strategies and comprehend content.
- Teachers debrief with whole class about the content and the skills — linguistic, meta-linguistic, meta-cognitive, comprehension, social, and cooperative learning skills — which they learned.

9. Consolidation of content and skills. Teachers use cross-cutting strategies to anchor knowledge, check for understanding, and assess individual student learning, through:
   - Writing for different purposes in different styles, and for reflection and summarizing what has been learned.
   - Instructional Conversations with whole class, small teams, individual students.
   - Cooperative Learning — a variety of methods (e.g. Roundtable, WriteAround, Tea Party, several Jigsaws, Numbered Heads Together, Cooperative Integrated Reading and Composition).
   - Teachers present and model questions and activities for students to formulate questions at different levels of complexity, and test them on peer teams.
   - Teachers incorporate social skills and teamwork development during partner and team activities.

10. Assessments
    - Teachers use monitoring charts (e.g., for teamwork, for ELL discourse, for use of new vocabulary) and show students how to use them for self-assessment and team assessment.
    - Performance assessments (e.g., student reflections, team presentations).
    - Portfolio contents (e.g., writing samples, individual products, reports)
    - Other assessments (e.g., team products, monthly tests, weekly quizzes).
    - State or district assessments.

Three Basic Premises Guiding These Lessons

Premise 1—100% Student Interaction: A feature that is perhaps the most critical for ELL success is the continuous constant production on oracy and literacy tasks. For every instructional and learning event, the students must produce and practice until there is evidence of mastery. For example, a teacher uses specific techniques such as "turn to your partner," choral responses, and others to ensure all ELLs are talking and practicing the new words; instead of round-robin reading, teachers use partner reading to ensure 100% time on reading for all students; instead of calling on one student for an answer, teachers use the Numbered-Heads-Together strategy, where all students discuss the answer and one number is called to represent the group. This method ensures that all students prepare each other to respond successfully.

Premise 2—Semantic Awareness: A school, classroom, and learning environment must be permeated with a mind-set that ELLs are learning words minute by minute. For example, a principal in a middle school ends her announcements with "the word of the day." She states the word twice, gives a definition, and uses it in a sentence. As she walks around school the rest of the day, the students stop her and give their own sentence with the word of the day. Another example is when teachers meet in interdisciplinary teams and identify sets of high utility words that cut across all content areas, and polysemous words such as *table, cell, power, radical,* and so on. They plan which words to teach on a weekly basis in order to ensure more than 12 exposures/encounters with a word in a variety of contexts.

Premise 3—The Explicit Teaching of Reading Comprehension: Explicit instruction for developing reading comprehension skills and strategies can be applied to other reading situations (Tierney & Readence, 2000; Slavin & Madden, 2001) such as content reading. The National Reading Panel (2000) found that comprehension strategy instruction, as opposed to comprehension skill practice (e.g., traditional skill work such as identifying main idea, cause-effect, fact-opinion) was important for students' reading growth. The features of explicit teaching include:

- **Relevance**: Students are made aware of the purpose of the skill or strategy—the why, when, how, and where of the strategy.
- **Definition**: Students are informed as to how to apply the skills by making public the skill or strategy, modeling its use, discussing its range of utility, and illustrating what it is not.

- **Guided practice**: Students are given feedback on their own use of the strategy or skill.
- **Self-regulation**: Students are given opportunities to try out the strategy for themselves and develop ways to monitor their own use of the strategy or skill.
- **Gradual release of responsibility**: The teacher initially models and directs the students' learning; as the lesson progresses, the teacher gradually gives more responsibility to the student.
- **Application**: Students are given the opportunity to try their skills and strategies in independent learning situations, including nonschool tasks.

The focus of the research and development proposed in this book is on translating the findings of explicit strategy instruction into practical, replicable techniques to make strategy instruction effective as a routine part of reading comprehension and English language development in science, social studies, math, and language arts classrooms with small or large numbers of ELLs.

The Research Base for the ExC-ELL 10-Step Lesson Framework

Each component of the lesson has been based on research. A synthesis of this research is included here so teachers and administrators can continue to pursue related research, conduct more profound studies, or use this information to write proposals that can fund their staff development programs or empirical studies of what works in their schools. The primary purpose, however, is to guide teachers through the development of their lessons once they have studied the background of each component.

Segmenting and Parsing Text. After reading a selected text, the teacher prepares it for the construction of meaning and for presenting the lesson. The teacher identifies the major ideas for students to construct and predicts where trouble spots may occur. Then teachers decide where to segment the text and where to stop the students' reading, and initiate a discussion toward the construction of meaning (Beck, McKeown, Hamilton, & Kucan, 1997; Graves, Cooke, & Laberge, 1983). For the ExC-ELL we've asked teachers to segment the text for their read-aloud portion, as well as the students' sections for partner reading and silent reading. They are to select the Tier 1, Tier 2, and Tier 3 words (some teachers call them "everyday words" and "technical words") for ELLs that have to be pre-taught explicitly or taught during and after reading (see below and Chapter 3 on vocabulary). Teachers also write some guiding questions for eliciting rich discussions after each segment. They also "condense and eliminate" extraneous information often found in basal texts in order to help students focus on important details and concepts fundamental to a subject area.

Vocabulary Strategies. Word knowledge correlates with comprehension (Beck et al., 2002; Samuels, 2002; Juel, 1988; Nagy & Anderson, 1984; Cunningham & Stanovich, 1998). For older struggling readers, the vocabulary in the books they read affects whether and how they achieve fluency and comprehension (Menon & Hiebert, 2003; Torgesen, Rashotte, Alexander, Alexander, & McFee, 2002). In other words, the size of a student's vocabulary bank predicts his or her level of reading comprehension. In today's terms this means that the number of words known also predicts how ELLs perform on high-stakes tests that call for any type of reading comprehension. Unless students know 85 to 95% of the words they are reading, comprehension will be stifled (Samuels, 2002). Vocabulary development strategies are of importance for all students, but especially for English language learners (Fitzgerald, 1995; García, 2000; Blachowicz & Fisher, 2000). Particularly promising vocabulary strategies include those described by Beck et al. (2002), Chamot & O'Malley (1996), Calderón, August, Slavin, Madden, Duran & Cheung (2005), Calderón & Minaya-Rowe (2003), and Padrón (1992). August, Calderón, & Carlo (2002) propose the use of cognates (taught with derivational and inflectional morphemes and other strategies) as effective vocabulary tools for Spanish-speaking ELLs. This is particularly important in schools where 95 to 98% of the students in middle and high schools are Hispanic. All teachers need to explicitly teach vocabulary before, during, and after reading for purposes of ensuring comprehension.

Activating Prior Knowledge. It is often said that good readers automatically bring prior knowledge to bear on new, related content, but poor readers may not do so. English language learners bring a different type of knowledge background from what is typical in a mainstream classroom. Although their experiences span a full range of possibilities, several studies have found young adolescents can be successfully taught to ask themselves what they already know about a given topic and then relate this to the current text, and this strategy increases comprehension (e.g., Hansen & Pearson, 1983; Dewitz, Carr, & Patberg, 1987). This strategy is widely used as part of the common KWL strategy, in which students are asked before reading what they already know about a topic (K), what they want to learn (W), and later, what they learned (L). Langer (1981) developed the PreReading Plan (PReP) technique to (1) give students an opportunity to generate what they know about a topic and to extend these ideas and evaluate them; and (2) to provide teachers with a procedure for assessing the adequacy of students' prior knowledge. ExC-ELL builds on these strategies by adding the analysis of word knowledge followed by ways teachers can elicit knowledge of concepts even if the students are very limited in their oral English.

Summarization. Having students summarize information they have read is one of the most consistently supported of all cognitive reading comprehension and study strategies (Brown & Day, 1983; Taylor & Beach, 1984; Palincsar & Brown, 1984; Rosenshine & Meister, 1994; Padrón & Waxman, 1988; Slavin & Madden, 2001). Armbruster, Anderson, and Ostertag (1987) successfully evaluated a particular form of summarization that analyzed social studies content into three boxes: Statement of a problem, actions taken to solve the problem, and results of the actions.

Statement of a Problem	Actions Taken to Solve a Problem	Results of the Actions

Malone & Mastropieri (1992) found summarization was made more effective if students with reading disabilities were also taught to monitor their own summaries using a checklist. One of the ExC-ELL strategies is for students to read a paragraph with a partner, and then orally summarize what was read. Another partner reading strategy is to read a paragraph and then formulate a test question that gets at the essence of that paragraph. At times, partners simply state, "This is what we found" in the paragraph; then, they summarize what they found in the complete page. Breaking up text into smaller chunks such as paragraphs seems to enable ELLs to process information more profoundly and recall it.

This is what we found:

Story Grammar/Text Formats. Another form of facilitated summarization that has been successfully evaluated is having students identify story grammar in narratives. That is, students identify the main characters, setting, problem, attempted problem solutions, and final solutions. Short and Ryan (1984) found this strategy to help students understand text. Idol (1987) and Idol and Croll (1987) had upper-elementary children use a "story map" that focused on the same story grammar elements, and this helped poor readers to comprehend the content. Pointing out characteristics of formats used by math, science, and social studies texts helps ELLs understand the focus of the lesson. ExC-ELL uses story maps and a variety of cognitive and semantic maps to help students comprehend and retain content.

Think-Alouds. Teachers' use of think-alouds is intended to help students examine and develop reading behaviors and strategies (Olshavsky, 1976–77; Flower & Hayes, 1980). As teachers describe their own thoughts about a text, students realize how and when to do the same. Think-alouds are used by ExC-ELL teachers for making predictions or showing how to develop hypotheses, describing one's visual images, sharing an analogy or showing how prior knowledge applies, verbalizing a confusing point or show how to monitor developing understandings, and demonstrating fix-up strategies.

Imagery. Gambrell and Bales (1986) had poor readers make pictures in their minds to understand the content of stories. Imagery has also been extensively studied as a mnemonic device for learning paired associates, as in learning names in other languages for objects (Pressley, Levin, & Delaney, 1982; Hattie, Biggs, & Purdie, 1996). ExC-ELL teachers will ask students to picture in their minds or to do quick draws of a science process or a historical sequence.

Fluency. Reading automaticity means decoding words with minimal attention to decoding and meaning of the words. Adult readers simply recognize the words instantly and accurately on sight. This type of processing frees the reader's conscious attention to comprehend or construct meaning from the text (Rasinski, 2000; Samuels, 2002). Not so for ELLs if they are not able to recognize the words. Word knowledge must also be accompanied by prosody. Prosody stresses the appropriate use of phrasing and expression (Dowhower, 1987). When readers embed appropriate volume, tone, emphasis, phrasing and other elements in oral expression, they are giving evidence of actively interpreting or constructing meaning from the passage—all of which must be taught for effective comprehension (Rasinski, 2000). In ExC-ELL teachers read aloud the beginning segment of a text to model reading fluency for students. Students then reread that segment aloud with their partners and continue to read the remainder of the text with the partner, keeping in mind the strategies modeled by the teacher. Partner read-aloud provides teachers opportunities to walk around and monitor and record the progress of the ELLs fluency. *(Please see EOP® fluency checklist attached to the observation/coaching protocol in Chapter 9.)*

Partner Reading. In partner reading, paired students take turns reading aloud to each other. Various forms of partner reading have been found to produce significant gains in fluency and comprehension (Eldredge, 1990; Koskinen & Blum, 1986; Slavin & Madden, 2001; Osborn, Lehr, & Hiebert, 2003). The partner provides support as needed with new words and reading fluency. Partner reading (1) provides students with many opportunities to practice reading, and (2) it provides students with guidance to how fluent readers read and with feedback to help them become aware of and correct their mistakes (Foorman & Mehta, 2002; Shanahan, 2002). Partner reading has been particularly effective with English language learners (Calderón, Hertz-Lazarowitz, & Slavin, 1998; Stevens et al., 1991) and both ELLs and Spanish as a second language learners in two-way bilingual programs (Calderón & Minaya-Rowe, 2003). In the ExC-ELL program teachers train students to use specific techniques and comprehension strategies for giving corrective feedback to each other. At times students read and look for answers to teacher questions; other times they formulate their own study questions or look for story grammar elements, critical events, or scientific process steps.

Question Generation. Another robust strategy for comprehension and vocabulary development is teaching young adolescents to generate their own questions about material they are reading. For example, Davey and McBride (1986) taught sixth graders to develop "think-type" questions as they read. This strategy helped students understand and recall the key ideas. King (1994) successfully used a similar strategy, and question generation is a central feature of reciprocal teaching. A variant focused in particular on vocabulary development is "Questioning the Author" (Beck & McKeown, 1991), in which students are taught a strategy for expository text in which they ask why an author included certain information or explanations. Charts with key verbs and question starters are used by ExC-ELL teachers to help students formulate higher-level questions of different types (e.g., knowledge, comprehension, application, synthesis, evaluation).

Transactional Strategies Instruction. The term "transactional strategies instruction" is used by Pressley & Woloshyn (1995) to refer to a set of related programs that were designed to teach a variety of reading comprehension strategies. The specific strategies emphasized include prediction, reacting to text, constructing images to represent ideas, checking back in the text, generating questions, and summarizing.

Predictions	Reactions to Text	Images for Ideas	Checking Back in the Text	Generating Questions	Summarizing

The term "coaching" has also been applied to these types of interaction events (Taylor, Pearson, Peterson, & Rodriguez, 2003). Instructional Conversations (Saunders, 2001; Saunders & Goldenberg, 1999) is another variation. Instructional Conversations (ICs) emphasize culturally responsive instruction where teachers help ELLs with language and knowledge-based differences as they interpret content presented in textbooks. The ExC-ELL project uses the ICs to engage students in the learning process by promoting rich language and academic involvement. The IC helps ELLs develop thinking and problem-solving skills, as well as with forming, expressing and exchanging ideas in speech and in writing (Saunders & Goldenberg, 1999). The enacted IC promotes learning by weaving together prior knowledge, experiences, and new concepts (Tharp & Yamauchi, 1994). We are using the following indicators: Classroom management, clear academic goal, higher rate of student talk, students' views and ideas, according to students' preferences, levels of understanding, and questioning and restating. The instructional elements in the IC enable the teacher to activate background knowledge while eliciting students' contributions and reasoning, and provide direct teaching when necessary in small teams or during a one-on-one. The conversational elements of the IC promote teacher responsiveness to students and less "known-answer" questions that allow for interactive discourse and general participation in a challenging but not threatening environment. These elements promote higher cognitive abilities, such as analysis, reflection, and critical thinking (Goldenberg, 1992/1993).

Graphic Organizers. A particularly promising form of summarization is having students represent ideas and connections among ideas in graphic forms. For example, Berkowitz (1986) had sixth graders write the title of a passage in the middle of a sheet of paper, and then add main ideas and supporting details around the passage title as they encountered them in the text. This strategy increased comprehension and retention of the content. Similarly, Baumann (1984) had sixth graders conceptualize the main idea of a paragraph as a tabletop, and then to identify supporting details as the table's legs. "Web" strategies, in which students link concepts as they read, have been widely used and generally found to be effective.

The Combination of Reading Strategies and Cooperative Learning. A variety of cooperative learning methods have been used to develop students' comprehension skills. For example, Dansereau (1988) have studied "cooperative scripts," in which students take turns summarizing and evaluating each other's summaries. Meloth and Deering (1992, 1994) found peers could help each other acquire cognitive strategies. Fantuzzo, Polite, and Grayson (1990) developed and evaluated reciprocal peer tutoring strategies to help students study complex material. Reciprocal Teaching is a method in which students work in cooperative learning groups to learn to make predictions, to generate questions about the text, to seek clarification when they did not understand, and to use summarization strategies (Palincsar & Brown, 1984). Cooperative Strategic Reading (Klingner & Vaughn, 1998) uses cooperative learning to teach skills such as previewing a text, brainstorming, predicting, identifying the most important information in a text, and then wrapping up what they have learned. Another study on Reciprocal Teaching was conducted specifically with ELLs in which the teacher and students engaged in dialogue as students were instructed in four specific comprehension monitoring strategies: (a) summarizing, (b) self-questioning, (c) clarifying, and (d) predicting (Padrón, 1992). She found these reciprocal teaching strategies could be successfully taught to ELLs when the teacher reads the text aloud to the students. When the teacher reads aloud, the teacher reading aloud helps ELLs learn the four comprehension strategies without having to wait until they learn to decode.

The Bilingual Cooperative Integrated Reading and Composition (BCIRC) (Calderón, Hertz-Lazarowitz, & Slavin, 1998) has teachers read aloud to model comprehension strategies, but also teaches students how to use the strategies as they read. BCIRC teaches students what to do before reading, during reading, and after reading a text in order to build comprehension and master the material by using a variety of cognitive strategies, including summarization, prediction, story grammar, graphic organizers, partner reading, and mental imagery. The Reading Wings/Alas Para Leer bilingual reading programs (Slavin & Madden, 2001) for upper elementary and middle schools nests the following activities into cooperative learning: listening comprehension through think-alouds, story structure analysis, vocabulary building, partner reading, story retelling, spelling, story-related writing, and partner checking activities. In each of the cooperative methods cited here, students are given specific guidance in how to help a partner or teammate learn the content and develop a strategy. In ExC-ELL, cooperative learning plays a central role in introducing strategy instruction to students.

Self-Regulation/Debriefing/Metacognition. Metacognitive strategies typically grouped under the term self-regulation can be taught and used as reading comprehension strategies (Paris & Paris, 2001). In one sense, all mindful use of cognitive reading comprehension strategies is self-regulation, but self-regulated learning goes beyond this to touch on motivation, self-evaluation, and other learning efforts. A large body of research has shown the achievement benefits of self-regulatory strategies such as goal setting (Schunk & Swartz, 1993), using self-verbalization to talk oneself through a problem (Schunk & Cox, 1986), and self-monitoring by recording one's progress (Zimmerman, Bonner, & Kovach, 1996).

ExC-ELL teachers are taught to debrief with their students after each instructional and cooperative learning event in order to clarify, anchor knowledge and strategies, and think about improving their strategies for next time.

Writing Builds Comprehension. There is evidence writing to learn can contribute to improved reading comprehension and content learning

(Boscolo & Mason, 2001; Pugalee, 2002; Spanier, 1992). Both discussion of texts and the production of texts are seen as important to developing content-area literacy and learning. Effective writing instruction means giving ELLs frequent opportunities to write, accompanied by feedback and ample opportunities to revise and edit, along with guidance in how to do so (Williams, 2003). Instead of dictations, short-answer writing activities, and other similar tasks that limit writing practice, ELLs need explicit strategies for writing associated with different types of texts.

Second-Language Learning. The strategies and programs in secondary schools that include reading comprehension strategies have been effective for the most part with mainstream students. A few programs have been widely tested with ELL populations, but mainly with one or two subject matter areas. To our knowledge, none have been tested with ELLs in middle and high school science, social studies, and language arts classrooms at the same schools. In order to adapt these to ELLs, we integrated second-language learning strategies within each of the 12 components based on the research findings to date (August & Hakuta, 1997; Bialystok & Hakuta, 1994; Cummins, 1984; Krashen, 1982).

The ExC-ELL project also evolved from the work being generated by ongoing longitudinal studies being conducted by the P.I.s and colleagues:

- OERI/IES five-year study "Effective Programs for ELL Literacy: ESL, Transition, and Two-Way Bilingual"—Johns Hopkins University (1999–2004).
- Five-year "Randomized Study of Structured English Immersion, Transitional Bilingual, and Two-Way Bilingual Programs (90–10; 70–30; 50–50)"—Johns Hopkins University's Center for Data-Driven Reform in Education (2003–2008).
- DELSS (NICHD/IES) five-year study "Inter-linguistic, Intra-linguistic, and Developmental Factors of ELL Reading"—Center for Applied Linguistics, Johns Hopkins, Harvard, Miami Universities (2000–2005).
- IES five-year randomized study "National Center for Data-Driven Reform in Education–The ELL Achievement Component"—Johns Hopkins University.

The ExC-ELL project also used the latest and most comprehensive findings from a two-year panel work on ELL literacy: The National Literacy Panel on Language Minority Children and Youth and the

Carnegie Panel on literacy on adolescent ELLs. The main author of this book is a member of both panels.

The ExC-ELL project also uses basic principles from sheltered English instruction (SEI) to develop the second-language needs of ELLs (King, Fagan, Bratt, & Baer, 1987; Chamot & O'Malley, 1994; Short, 1994; Shaw, Ovando, & Collier, 1998; Echevarria, Vogt, & Short, 2000). The key components of SEI are lesson preparation, comprehensibility, lesson delivery, and interaction. SEI is scaffolded and mediated to provide refuge from the linguistic demands of English as a second-language (L2) discourse, which is beyond the current level of comprehension of the students. The theoretical underpinning SEI is language acquisition enhanced through meaningful use and interaction. SEI can be described as a melding of elements of language acquisition principles and elements of quality teaching (Echevarria & Graves, 1998). It is also influenced by sociocultural theory because it occurs within social and cultural contexts. This approach facilitates a high level of student involvement and interaction in the classroom. Teachers present material in patterns related to their students' language and culture as well as that of the school. Through this approach, students learn new material through the lens of their own language and culture (Valdes, 1996).

Assessment. Assessment should work in partnership with teaching and learning, particularly as it relates to differentiated learning and differentiated assessment practices (Gottlieb, 2006; Tierney & Readence, 2000). In the delivery of classroom instruction, language proficiency standards and academic content standards must merge and commingle if we are to asses ELL progress (Gottlieb, 2006). ExC-ELL teachers learned about the following assessment strategies to use in conjunction with their teaching: performance assessment, portfolios, anecdotal records, and for assessing team products, cooperative learning methods, and writing. Checklists and rubrics are also used to help students practice self-assessment and peer assessment.

First Steps in Lesson Design for Integrating Vocabulary, Reading, and Content

Teachers use the first five components of the lesson plan as described in the beginning of this chapter to plan their lesson. First they select the *standard or objective*. This helps them to do backward planning, where the outcome is determined first, then the lesson is designed.

To measure the outcome, *student assessments* are selected or developed next. Once the outcomes are determined, teachers preview the text to select, condense, eliminate unnecessary information, and segment the text for orchestrating daily activities. This is called *parsing* the text. A text can be a textbook chapter, a worksheet, a long story, anything the students are about to read. Not all texts need parsing. Some are short and trite enough already. You would not parse a poem either. However, when it is "impossible to cover" all the information in a chapter or a whole book, it is wise and practical to parse. It is better that students learn basic concepts profoundly than try to cover too much superficially.

Once the text is parsed, the teacher writes a *summary* to make sure the main ideas they want to cover are there. This summary can also be shared with the students as an anticipatory set, during the lesson to steer them in the right direction, or after the lesson as an exemplar for writing their own summaries. The teacher summaries also help to determine what graphics, films, pictures, objects, or other ancillary materials will be needed to build *student background.* After the first day of instruction, there will be a need to *review concepts* from the previous lesson, and those can be built in from the beginning or the space left blank until you know what the students need to review from the previous day.

The next chapter lays out how to select and teach vocabulary that is appropriate not just for ELLs but also for all students in a classroom. Subsequently, the chapter on reading comprehension uses questions to think about what the focus will be for a particular lesson and what to do before, during, and after students read a selection. The ensuing chapters provide lessons for math, science, language arts, and interdisciplinary units.

Summary

✓ There are 3 basic premises that guide instruction for ELLs and low-level readers: (1) ensuring 100% oral use, reading practice, and written production of new words and concepts; (2) establishing a mind-set of semantic awareness; and (3) the explicit teaching of reading comprehension skills germane to each content area.

✓ There are 5 components that assist teachers of science, social studies, math, and language arts in planning lessons that integrate vocabulary and reading comprehension skill development.

✓ There are 5 components that assist content teachers in planning the delivery of their content and the way students will interact with that content to process and learn critical information.

✓ There is a strong research base for each of the 10 components. While it is essential for teachers to use the 10 components, empirical studies indicate that they are adjustable to a teacher's creativity and subject area.

3

Vocabulary Development

The Foundation for Reading in the Content Areas

Selecting Words to Teach

The selection of words to preteach was based on research by Beck and colleagues (Beck, McKeown, & Kucan, 2002) as well as on the work of the Vocabulary Improvement Project (Carlo et al., 2005), the BCIRC study (Calderón, Hertz-Lazarowitz & Slavin, 1998), and the Transition from Spanish into English study (Calderón et al., 2005). Beck and colleagues have developed a systematic method of selecting vocabulary to teach to students. Words are grouped into three tiers, and words in Tier 2 are those targeted for instruction. Tier 2 words include (1) words that have importance and utility (they are characteristic of mature language users and appear frequently across a variety of domains), (2) words that have instructional potential (words that can be worked with in a variety of ways so that students can build rich representations of them and their connections to other words and concepts, and (3) words for which students already have conceptual understanding (words for which students understand the general concept but provide precision and specificity in describing the concept). Tier 1 words are words English-speaking students already know and Tier 3 words are words students are unlikely to know but are also words that are not frequently used across a variety of domains. The approach to teaching the words in each tier is predicated on four dimensions: nature of the word (is it concrete or can it be demonstrated), its cognate status, depth of word meaning, and utility (Beck, McKeown, & Kucan, 2002).

Tier 1 Words for ELLs. We take it for granted that native English speakers know most Tier 1 words, but this is not the case for English language learners. Many Tier 1 words may be unknown to English language learners and key to the comprehension of a written passage. For Tier 1 words, ELLs typically know the concept in their primary language but not the label in English. For example, a Tier 1 word might be *butterfly.* This is a word that English language learners may not know, but it can be easily taught during a text presentation and discussion by pointing to a picture of a butterfly and asking the students to say it three times. Another Tier 1 word might be *bug.* Words like *bug* (insect) or *march* (move like a soldier) may be easily instructed during text discussion by pointing to a picture of a *bug* or *marching* in place, but because the words are polysemous (have multiple meanings), they merit further instruction, and this can be accomplished in oral language activities that follow the text discussion (Calderón et al., 2005).

TIER 1

Words that ELLs need for everyday speech, for academic conversations and explanations, and for scaffolding more complicated text.

- Basic words for which students know concept and label in the primary language but need English label (e.g., *find, search, guest, tooth, answer*).
- Simple idioms are basic expressions that ELLs are unlikely to know (e.g., *make up your mind; let's hit the books; once upon a time; sit up*).
- Connectors (e.g., *so, if, then, however, finally*).

There are some Tier 1 words that cannot be demonstrated and are not polysemous, but students will need to know them also (e.g., *uncle*). A simple explanation of the word's meaning during the story reading will suffice, or if the teacher and students are bilingual, a translation is sufficient. Simple idioms and everyday expressions (e.g., *make up your mind; let's hit the books; once upon a time*) are also Tier 1 words, and teachers will need to explain the word meaning to students. Some Tier 1 words are cognates with a language like Spanish (*family/familia; preparation/preparación*); the cognates in this category consist of words that are high-frequency words in Spanish and English; they do not require substantial instruction because students know the word meanings in Spanish. (The teacher merely states the English cognate, and students provide the Spanish cognate, or the teacher provides the English cognate, and the students say both the English word and Spanish cognate.) False cognates also need to be pointed out by the teacher and the correct translation given (*rope/ropa, soap/sopa*). The word *assist* is usually translated as *asistir*, but the correct translation is *atender*, and *attend* means *asistir*. Yet *asistencia* means *assistance*, but *attendance* is not *atendencia* (this word does not exist), and it is also correct to say *asistencia*. Confusing enough? We call these *polysemous cognates*. They can be either true or false cognates, depending on the context.

Tier 2 Words for ELLs. These are words that have importance and utility because they are in grade-level texts. Unfortunately, these do not receive as much attention as Tier 1 and Tier 3 words because ESL teachers typically teach Tier 1, and mainstream teachers focus on Tier 3 (content key) words. It's our hypothesis that the lack of explicit instruction of Tier 2 words is what keeps ELLs from moving on to Tier 3 words and thus developing reading comprehension of content texts.

Tier 2 words can be worked with in a variety of ways so students can build rich representations of them and make connections to content words and concepts. These are also words for which students understand the general concept but need to learn to provide precision and specificity in describing the concept.

Some Tier 2 words are those tiny words that make comprehension difficult for ELLs, such as *so, at, into, within, by, if, then*. Others are sometimes clustered to connote certain usage, constructs, or "ways of talking about school stuff," as one teacher calls them. They are also called transition words. These are helpful to compare and contrast, to describe or give examples. The box below has some examples.

In addition, many Tier 2 words are cognates (in this Tier they are high-frequency words in Spanish and low-frequency words in English), and children whose first language shares cognates with English will have a head start with these words. Words in Spanish parallel words in English, such as *digestion/digestion, coincidence/ coincidencia, industrious/industrioso*, and *fortunate/afortunado*. Many

Spanish speakers will know both the concept and an approximation of the label in English. If they don't know the meaning in either language, both can be taught together. This category also includes less common idioms and metaphors that are key to making inferences.

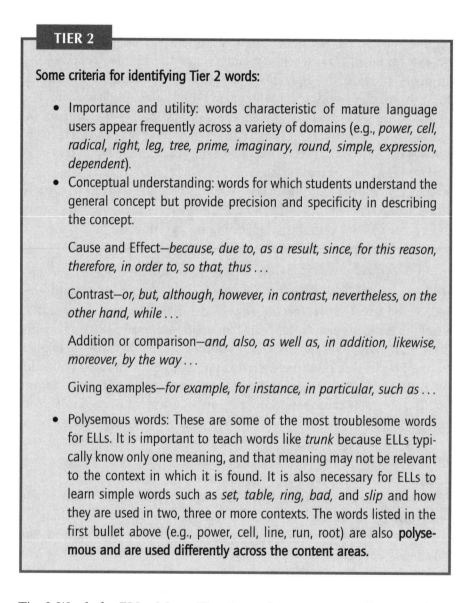

TIER 2

Some criteria for identifying Tier 2 words:

- Importance and utility: words characteristic of mature language users appear frequently across a variety of domains (e.g., *power, cell, radical, right, leg, tree, prime, imaginary, round, simple, expression, dependent*).
- Conceptual understanding: words for which students understand the general concept but provide precision and specificity in describing the concept.

  Cause and Effect—*because, due to, as a result, since, for this reason, therefore, in order to, so that, thus . . .*

  Contrast—*or, but, although, however, in contrast, nevertheless, on the other hand, while . . .*

  Addition or comparison—*and, also, as well as, in addition, likewise, moreover, by the way . . .*

  Giving examples—*for example, for instance, in particular, such as . . .*

- Polysemous words: These are some of the most troublesome words for ELLs. It is important to teach words like *trunk* because ELLs typically know only one meaning, and that meaning may not be relevant to the context in which it is found. It is also necessary for ELLs to learn simple words such as *set, table, ring, bad,* and *slip* and how they are used in two, three or more contexts. The words listed in the first bullet above (e.g., power, cell, line, run, root) are also **polysemous and are used differently across the content areas.**

Tier 3 Words for ELLs. Many Tier 3 words are cognates because they are specific to certain content areas (e.g., *osmosis, photosynthesis, peninsula*). However, students may not know the actual concept or process; therefore they need to be pretaught along with the concept. Sometimes, the students may have partial knowledge of a concept or word (fractions) and need details or specificity. If possible, Tier 3 words that are not demonstrable or are cognates can be translated or briefly explained in the first language. In this category we also include others that may not be essential to understanding the main points of the text. These can be explained briefly to the students, but they don't have to master these words.

TIER 3

Low-frequency words in English.

These are the words that are limited to specific domains, such as social studies, math, language arts, or science. Although they are low-frequency words, they are very important for understanding content. For instance: *lathe, isotope, peninsula, osmosis, polysemy, hyperbole* [all cognates].

- Cognates are words in two or more languages that sound almost the same or are spelled the same (for instance in English, Spanish, and French we find words such as *telephone/teléfono/téléphone; the radio, el radio, le radio; education/la educación/l'éducation*).
- Literate Spanish speakers have a great advantage over monolingual English speakers with Tier 3 words because many cognates are high-frequency words in Spanish but low-frequency words in English (e.g., *coincidence/coincidencia, absurd/absurdo, concentrate/concéntrate, and fortunate/afortunado*).
- However, some students will need to learn the concept or specificity for some cognates (e.g., *democracy/democracia*).
- Polysemous cognates and false cognates (e.g., *mass/masa or misa; attend a meeting/asistir a una junta; assist someone/atender a alguien/asistencia; round/redondo/vuelta round off/redondear*).

Of course cognates and polysemous words can be either Tier 1, 2, or 3. It depends on the difficulty of the word or the background knowledge of the student. By the same token, selecting words for the three tiers will also depend on the subject, grade level, and student background knowledge. ***There are no lists for Tiers 1, 2, and 3.*** Each classroom will be different. Each group of students will be different. Each will require an analysis of the words to be taught before, during, and after reading.

It is important to preselect words to teach before, during, and after reading to focus on the most important concepts from the standards and basic knowledge that will make a difference in the student's test results. As the students delve into the text, there will be other words you might not have even thought about. These can be collected and pretaught the following day, or they can be taught quickly without interrupting the reading too long. The following section describes ways teachers and students like to conduct word study activities in the context of learning content and preparing for exams.

Preteaching Vocabulary

Preteaching vocabulary is critical to comprehension. Before students read a text or a teacher reads a text aloud to the students or a teacher lectures, it is vital to preteach 6 or 7 words that are key to comprehending that text or lecture. There may be many words ELLs do not know in each subject area. Therefore, the selection of those 6–7 words to preteach in all content classrooms needs special attention. Teachers can select 2 or 3 words from each tier each day, as the students progress through a textbook or combination of reading, discussions, lectures, summarizing of content.

Preteaching vocabulary is a seven-step process. It is different from the process used by Beck and colleagues because these steps integrate second-language strategies.

1. The teacher says the word in English (and in the primary language in bilingual classrooms).

2. The teacher states the word in context from the text.

3. The teacher provides a definition or key definitions from the dictionary (not the students—they may have partially correct or wrong definitions).

4. The teacher provides another example of the word in a way that clarifies the word's meaning (in student-friendly terms).

5. The teacher asks students to repeat the word at least 3 times to build a phonological representation of the word.

6. The teacher ensures 100% of the students become "engaged with the word" through oral language activities. The production activity can be carried out with a partner. For instance, the

teacher might say, "Tell your partner about a time you were *mesmerized.*" After a minute of sharing with partners, the teacher asks two or three students to share what their partners said. "Turn to your partner" and "tell me what your partner said" ensure 100% production by all students because all are using the word at the same time and hearing it several times from others. When they have to report to the teacher what their partners said, they need to apply it again from a different reference point, a different context, using it with related words and phrases. This discourse sequence helps ELLs anchor their knowledge of the word. It helps non-ELLs achieve higher levels of specificity. It also develops listening and paraphrasing skills, third-person pronoun-verb agreement (My partner says . . .), and other grammatical structures.

7. They say the word again or the whole sentence where it is found.

Here is an example of how teaching the word *revolution* might look through the seven steps:

1. *Revolution.* Say *revolution* 3 times with me.

2. The text says: The revolution was set in motion with a sequence of actions from 1763 to 1783.

3. The dictionary defines it as the overthrow of a government or social system with another taking its place. Another meaning I see here is "movement of a body, a star or planet in a circle." The revolution of the earth around the sun takes how long?

4. My children love pizza. But, if I have to eat pizza again this weekend, I will start a revolution!

5. Say *revolution* with me 3 times.

6. What would make you start a revolution? Share with your partner. (After 1 minute) What did your partner say?

7. Let's say (or spell) the word.

100% Engagement. There are many other ways of getting students engaged with a word. It does not always have to be a "think-pair-share" activity. Students can respond chorally or in popcorn style (students call out answers as they think of them), or by applause or thumbs-up signals, as in the following examples.

1. Answer teacher questions by giving reasons or examples:

2. If you are walking into a dark room, you need to do it cautiously. Why?

3. Using critical thinking skills while learning words. Selecting or making choices.
    Which of these things would be integers? Answer in a complete sentence.
    – a positive number or a fraction?
    – a negative number or a decimal?
    – a zero or a percent?

4. Thinking about specificity when using adjectives, verbs, or concepts.
    – Applaud if you hear an adjective:
      – affected
      – few
      – mainly
      – farther
    – Applaud if the name you hear belongs to a U.S. president:
      – James Monroe
      – Martin Sheen
      – Benjamin Franklin
      – Thomas Jefferson

When teachers use strategies such as these to preteach vocabulary, they are also teaching or reviewing other skills, concepts, and/or metacognitive strategies. With the example of the word *integer* students need to listen carefully, compare two responses, and choose the most appropriate one. They have to think quickly, make inferences, and respond. The teacher can ask for complete sentence responses, where ELLs can practice answering long strands of discourse, scaffolded by the teacher's phrases. This ensures appropriate answers, the use of "would be" and other more sophisticated patterns. (A positive number *would be* an example of an integer.) Responding in complete sentences creates a sense of confidence and self-efficacy in the ELLs as their responses become more and more sophisticated.

Developing Vocabulary Through Discourse Around Text

Vocabulary is also developed through ongoing dialogue between the teacher and students about the text during teacher and student reading. Reading begins with the teacher reading aloud the first two paragraphs or so of a text. During the read-aloud, the teacher uses different types of questions, stopping at specific intervals in the text to ellicit discussion and teach more words "on the run." Different methods are used depending on the nature of the word (is it concrete, or can it be demonstrated?), its cognate status, depth of word meaning, and utility. Strategies for teaching English as a second language such as the following can be used to teach words on the run. The use of pantomime and gestures, showing pictures and real objects, and doing quick draws on the board can be used to quickly explain what a word means.

Questions can also help prompt students to talk about ideas using the target words. Questions have to be carefully crafted ahead of time. Some questions elicit one-word responses or are likely to elicit only sparse responses. There are also questions that help students move from using just pictures and background knowledge to more elaborated responses tied to the text. Other questions call for more thinking and elaboration. The graph on page 38 is one example of a tool often distributed to the students for constructing and answering questions.

Oral Language Activities for Building Vocabulary

The language development activities that follow reading are based in large part on the words the story has provided. Different stories, chapters, texts lend themselves to different kinds of oral activities that help further language ease. Nevertheless, the key focus is on developing conceptual knowledge about the words and reinforcing labels for the word. The following examples focus on different syntactic and semantic features of English.

How Students Learn and Remember Homonyms

Students can use Venn diagrams to compare and contrast words across subjects or to learn homonyms. Seeing how words are used across content areas helps them remember their multiple meanings. For example, students can place the words and provide a mini definition to words such as *pi* and *pie.*

Figure 3.1

APPLYING BLOOM'S TAXONOMY OF COGNITIVE PROCESS—5			
THINKING PROCESS	*USEFUL VERBS*	*SAMPLE QUESTIONS STEMS*	*POTENTIAL ACTIVITIES AND PRODUCTS*
S Y N T H E S I S	Create Invent Compose Predict Plan Construct Design Imagine Improve Propose Devise Formulate	Can you design a…to…? What is a possible solution to…? What would happen if…? If you had access to all resources, how would you deal with… How would you devise your own way to…? How many ways can you…? Can you create new and unusual uses for…? Can you develop a proposal that would…? How would you compose a song about…? Can you write a new recipe for a tasty dish?	• Invent a machine to do a specific task. • Design a building. • Create a new product. Give it a name and plan a marketing campaign. • Write about your feelings in relation to… • Write a TV show, play puppet show, role play, song, or pantomime about… • Design a record, book, or magazine cover for… • Devise a way to… • Create a language code. • Sell an idea to a billionaire. • Compose a rhythm or put new words to a known melody.

Figure 3.2

Place these words and add mini definition:
sum some; pi pie; plane plain; complement compliment

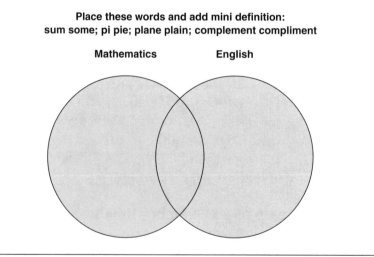

Graphic organizers are great tools for ELLs for organizing information to be learned and also for using the new words in extended
discourse through oral summaries or retell.

How Students Learn and
Remember Polysemous Words

After the students have been introduced to polysemous words in the preteaching phase, they will need an opportunity to use them at least 12 times before we can say they have mastered each word (Stahl, 2005).

We say that mastery of any word for ELLs means knowing these six aspects:

1. How to decode it.

2. How to pronounce it correctly.

3. The meaning for comprehending the immediate text context.

4. Other important meanings.

5. How to spell the word.

6. How to use it correctly while writing summaries.

An activity that helps ELLs learn polysemous words that cuts across several content areas is to provide a list of these words and have them discuss and write sentences with each. For example:

Write as many sentences as you can using each word for math, science, social studies, and/or language arts:

PRIME	IMAGINARY	LEG
POWER	RIGHT	CELL
RADICAL	SET	ROUND

How Students Learn and
Remember Words by Using Affixes

Team or individual written exercises help reinforce word meaning, apply multiple meanings of words, as well as analyze and play with prefixes, suffixes, and parts of speech in sentences, as in the example below. These exercises can also be given as homework or as sponge activities when students have finished their work. Some teachers have these handy for times when there are still five minutes before the bell rings!

These are other prefixes and suffixes that lend themselves to similar activities:

Figure 3.3

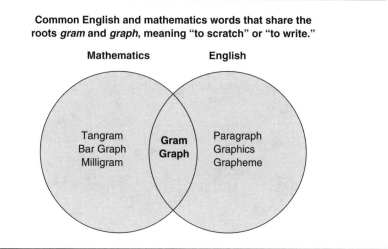

Common English and mathematics words that share the roots *gram* and *graph*, meaning "to scratch" or "to write."

Math Prefixes:

bi	co	contra	equi	kilo
mono	multi	octa	peri	quad
rect	semi	tri		

These are examples for language arts:

Suffixes of the Week	*Meaning*	*Examples*
Let	Small	Starlet, booklet, leaflet
Ant	One who	Migrant, merchant, assistant, dominant
Ly	Similar to	Brotherly, neighborly, sickly, strangely
Prefixes of the Week	*Meaning*	*Examples*
In	Not	Incompetent, incomplete, inability, inhumane
Fore	First part	Forewarned, foresight, forecast
Inter	Across	International, interstate, interview
Ad	To	Adapt, addict, admonish, admit

Other Strategies Students Like to Use to Remember Words

Students like to use props. They like sticky tabs, Post-it notes, color markers, color dots, pens in several colors. They underline, highlight, box, circle, and write over new words. They underline with red the words that are the hardest; in yellow those they "kinda know"; and in green for those they already know.

Students like to make lists. They draw lines down a sheet as follows:

Red Words	Yellow Words	Green Words

Students like to work in pairs. To study a word they can either

- Draw a cartoon using the word.
- Design a creative way of representing the word.
- Invent a mnemonic device to remember the word, such as a brief chant, rhyme, rap, joke, or even a Shakespearean iambic pentameter stanza.
- Try to come up with as many synonyms for that word as possible.
- Try to come up with as many antonyms for that word as possible.
- Using all the words of the week, develop word games to play with other pairs.
- Put words on cards with clues and challenge another pair of students.
- Act the word out, or invent a motion to match the meaning, play charades with another pair.

Students love the word polysemous. They like to

- Locate polysemous words in the text.
- Go to the dictionary and find the multiple meanings of a word.
- Challenge other teams with multiple meanings.
- Invent a rap, chant, song, or a silly sentence using the multiple meanings, such as *"The trunk with the elephant's trunk was found under the tree trunk and put in the car trunk along with our swimming trunks."*

Students like word searches/puzzles in teams. They like to

- Find compound words, prefixes, suffixes in the text.
- Break up compound words and put together other words with each part.
- Use affixes such as *gram, photo, graph, geo, phon, cycl, deci, scribe, vid, dyna* and say in which subject they would be most likely to find that word.
- List as many key words as they can remember from a chapter.
- Challenge other teams to find several key words in a text, while timing them.
- Writing meaningful sentences (where the meaning is embedded in the sentence) with words such as *metaphor,* for example: "Juan used a metaphor, a figure of speech, a sensory symbol, a most poetic way to tell Rosa he liked her when he said, 'You are a true rose.'"

Working in pairs or teams of four makes learning fun and easy. Teachers like cooperative learning because they can monitor student learning much more easily. They can also conduct instructional conversations where students are guided to use the words they are learning, to discuss the topics they are studying, and to ask the teacher questions. Ways of organizing effective cooperative learning strategies that are specific to literacy development are further described in the next chapters.

How teachers like teaching words

There are ongoing activities designed to review words from previous lessons and help students listen for and use words outside of the class. Games are used to promote word use outside of class. Some activities can be designed to conduct with parents, older siblings, or for self-review, such as additional passages with the vocabulary learned that day. A classroom where there is semantic awareness has word walls that contain pictures of the words and labels or words organized by category. Student writing is posted, as well as posters containing reminders about grammar, syntax, and cognates. This chapter ends with a sample of "Teachers' Favorite Vocabulary Activities" we have collected in middle and high schools.

For Preteaching Vocabulary Before Reading

1. List of technical words and everyday words are on the board.

2. The teacher reads the words and gives quick definitions or explanations.

3. Students say each word 3 times.

4. The teacher reads aloud from the beginning of a new chapter or text and asks students to visualize as she reads.

5. Teacher emphasizes words as she reads, adding meaning to the context.

6. Students raise their hands each time they hear a new word.

7. Students later work with words in various ways—writing sentences, doing word puzzles, and writing summaries using as many new words as possible.

For Reviewing and Preteaching Words in Ongoing Reading

1. List of *technical words* and *everyday words* are on board from yesterday.

2. The teacher reads aloud from the beginning of a new chapter or text while students circle unknown *technical words* and underline *everyday words*.

3. Teacher asks each team to give words from both categories as he lists them on the board next to yesterday's words.

4. Teacher says the word and gives a quick definition or example. Students later work with words in a variety of ways.

For Reviewing Words With Numbered Heads Together

1. Students number off from 1 to 4.

2. The teacher gives them a typed list of Tier 1, 2, and 3 words learned that week.

3. Students must make sure everyone in the team knows the definition, spelling, pronunciation, and how to use the words in a sentence.

4. The teacher calls a number; the corresponding student is given a word and must answer for the team by saying it, spelling it, and using it in a sentence.

For Reviewing Words With Expert Jigsaw

1. Teacher gives each team a different set of laminated index cards with vocabulary words on one side and definitions on the other.

2. Students must make sure everyone in the team knows the definition, spelling, pronunciation, and how to use it in a sentence.

3. Then, every 3 minutes two students go to a different table to teach and test those students.

For Reviewing Words Before a Test

1. Students form a "Conga Line" or "Tea Party Line" or "Texas Two-Step Line."

2. They bring lists of words and stand in front of a partner.

3. With partner number one, they practice using words in sentences or reviewing definitions before their test.

4. When the music starts, they move to the next partner to practice more words.

5. They continue changing partners and studying words for about 5 minutes.

For Reviewing Words With Vocabulary Roundtable

1. Each team uses only one paper and one pencil.

2. In round-robin style, each student writes one word learned that week, passes the paper to the right, the next student writes a different one, and so on, until teacher calls time. The team with the most words wins.

For Reviewing Words With Vocabulary Write-Around

1. Each student has one paper and writes a sentence using a word, passes the paper to the right. Reads the one passed from the left, and adds a sentence with a new word.

For Reviewing With Vocabulary Amazing Race

1. Students are given a polysemous word to look up in the dictionary and thesaurus.

2. They must write 3 or more sentences using a different meaning.

3. Once the teacher approves the sentences, they are given an envelope with scrambled definitions and words to put together.

4. Once the teacher approves that the definition, they have another task using 5 words correctly (e.g., compose a song; make a poster).

For Identifying Words to Reteach

1. A parking lot poster is placed close to the classroom door with a Post-it pad next to the poster.

2. Students write unfamiliar words they encounter during class or in homework assignments on the Post-its and place them on the parking lot.

3. Teacher discusses each word at the end of the period or begins the next day explaining the words and concepts.

Summary

✓ Vocabulary must be explicitly taught to ELLs if they are to catch up to grade-level standards.

✓ Vocabulary instruction must also be part of a comprehensive language and literacy program across the content areas.

✓ It is important to preselect words to teach before, during, and after reading to focus on the most important concepts from the standards, and basic knowledge that will make a difference in the students' test results.

✓ Explicit instruction on word knowledge consisting of phonemic, phonological, and morphemic awareness, decoding, and understanding of the multiple meanings of the words occurs in the context of teaching reading and using content texts.

✓ Language development is accelerated through reading, discussing, writing about texts—after Tier 1, 2, and 3 vocabulary has been explicitly taught.

4

Teaching Reading Comprehension and Content

How Is Teaching Reading Different for ELLs in Secondary Schools?

Reading in the content areas has typically meant "reading to learn," as differentiated from beginning reading instruction, which has been referred to as "learning to read" (McKenna & Robinson, 1990). Content area literacy for ELLs refers to reading and writing to learn concepts from textbooks, novels, magazines, e-mail, electronic messaging, Internet materials, or Internet sites so they can keep up with their subject matter and pass the high-stakes tests. It also means learning to read these texts critically, forming opinions, and responding appropriately orally and in writing. It means keeping up with all subjects and daily course work. It also means being part of the culture of the Internet in order to access information, evaluate contents quickly, and synthesize information for various classes. English language learners, like all other students, need to understand the languages of disciplines like biology, algebra, government, and English literature—for each is a different language in itself. This is definitely not easy to accomplish! Neither for ELLs nor for their teachers! Nevertheless, this is what all teachers must strive for.

The problem with ESL only. Expository or informational texts have their own language and organizational format. They vary considerably across subject matter. Scientists, mathematicians, historians, linguists speak and write differently when explaining their domain. Each domain has its set of nomenclature and semantic preferences for nesting that terminology. For years the field of second-language teaching has espoused the concept of providing "comprehensible input" (Krashen, 1981), where teachers modify their speech and use visuals and other techniques to make instruction comprehensible to ELLs. While it is important for ELLs to understand the teacher, most sheltered content teachers or ESL content teachers simplify their language to the point where students are learning very few words, especially when it comes to subject matter.

It is quite likely most ELLs were primarily exposed to narrative genre as commonly used in ESL or language arts. Their English as a second-language instruction might have consisted of only simple oral language patterns (e.g., "This is a. . ."; "I have a . . ." and simple phrase responses) or reading short, choppy sentences. The words and grammatical structures that show rhetorical or narrative connections between ideas are often eliminated (Fillmore & Snow, 2002). English language learners' basic terminology and syntactical and discourse structures for the subject matter you are teaching may be very limited or non-existent. If so, then these students have a lot of catching up to do. Without additional reading and language development support from their mainstream content teachers, student comprehension remains at a shallow level—a surface comprehension level.

Notwithstanding, one must always keep an oxymoron in mind—provide comprehensible input and rich vocabulary. It is most challenging but critically important for teachers to balance comprehensible input with rich vocabulary.

Problems with too much sheltering. Publishers of sheltered instruction or content-based ESL textbooks use readability formulas that keep ELLs reading below second- or third-grade levels even in secondary schools. Important topics and concepts are reduced to a couple of sentences, devoid of detail. We have observed sheltered content classrooms where out of desperation for lack of detail, students are asked to go to search in encyclopedias. The students have no recourse but to copy straight out of the pages without really understanding the basic concepts.

In contrast, instruction that provides an in-depth, long-term focus on a specific domain not only improves general vocabulary but also improves reading comprehension. Instead of attempting to "cover" a lot of information, opportunities to probe profoundly into meaningful texts help *all* students, not just ELLs, experience deep comprehension and critical thinking.

Problems with too much phonics. Phonics programs in middle and high schools are fine as tools for ELLs that have low literacy skills in their first language. They also help more advanced ELLs that need to hear and distinguish the phonemes (sounds) and morphemes (smallest units of meaning) of English. However, phonics and decoding programs beyond 20 days have a downward spiral effect (Kamil, 2006). In other words, after 20 or so days of exposure to phonics only, there is no positive effect on students. Often, these programs focus only on sounds and not word knowledge. That means that students are parroting sounds devoid of meaning and sense to them. Along with phonics instruction, students need opportunities to practice those decoding skills with real texts, word study, and real discussions.

Problems with dense texts. School curricula, administrators, or teachers usually dictate or believe that the complete textbook be "covered." As teachers rush through the pages and content, ELLs and low-level readers are left behind. Because it is important for all students to engage with this type of text, a better option is to parse the text. To parse a text, teachers select the chapters or pages from a chapter all the basic information that addresses the district's standards. The fluff is left out. Kauai teachers defined parsing as "condensing and eliminating." After parsing texts for the week, they proceeded to select the vocabulary tiers, the reading comprehension skills that better suited that genre, and then the consolidation activities that would ensure students learned all the material selected. At first teachers were reluctant to cut out a lot, but as their students experienced more and more success, the teachers became comfortable with parsing.

A comprehensive approach. The more exposure ELLs have to explicit instruction of vocabulary, reading skills, and in-depth focus on a specific domain, the more improvement on reading fluency and motivation to learn that subject. It has to become "a vicious cycle" where vocabulary, reading comprehension, writing using the same words, and further reading and learning of more words are happening on a daily basis.

Figure 4.1   Reciprocal Effects

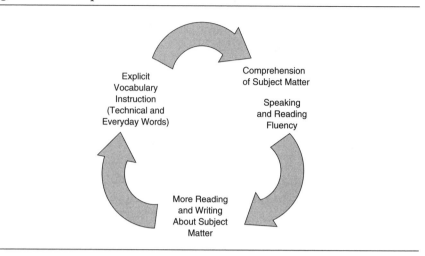

Lesson Planning for Integrating Vocabulary, Reading and Content

Teachers use the first 5 components of the lesson plan described in Chapter 2 to plan their lesson. First they select the standard or objective. This helps them to do backwards planning, where the outcome is determined first, then the lesson designed. To measure the outcome, student assessments are selected or developed next. Once the outcomes are determined, teachers preview the text to select, condense, eliminate unnecessary information, and segment the text for orchestrating daily activities.

After parsing and writing a summary, teachers can begin planning the reading comprehension part of the lesson by using a set of questions such as the following to work the text they have selected:

1. **Semantic awareness.**

   Which Tier 1, 2, and 3 words will I teach that will help them understand the main aspects of the text selection?

   Which techniques will I use to teach each one?

   How can I make sure students interact with each word at least 5 times prior to the lesson? And use the words 7 or more times during the lesson?

2. **Connecting students' prior knowledge with new knowledge.**

   Is the text appropriate, or do I parse it or find another?

   What do the students know about this topic? How can I find out?

What type of motivation and props can I use to connect to what we are about to read and learn?

3. **Metacognitive awareness.**

   Which reading strategies are most appropriate for comprehending this text?

   How do I present them in my read-aloud?

   Which is the best activity for the students to practice these skills?

   How will I debrief what they have learned?

4. **Active and engaged reading.**

   What are the best sections for partner reading?

   What strategy should I use for partner reading?

   How can I make sure they use the new vocabulary?

   Is there a graphic or cognitive organizer they can use?

   What follow-up cooperative learning strategy should I use to consolidate knowledge and develop more language skills?

5. **Ample discussions to anchor domain knowledge.**

   What are my questions for *before reading?*

   During reading, where do we stop and debrief?

   What are my debriefing questions for the final discussion *after reading?*

6. **Assessments.**

   How should I test their content knowledge? What is the best genre for writing up the content they have learned?

   What evidence of vocabulary, grammar, critical thinking and other skills do I want them to exhibit?

   What rubrics should I use?

   How will I test vocabulary?

   Other types of assessments fit here?

Preparing for Reading

The standard, objective, and purpose for reading and learning and how students will be graded are posted on the chalkboard. In other words, objectives, rubrics, and evaluation criteria are posted and introduced before the lesson begins.

Lists of Tier 1, 2, and 3 words are also posted. Teachers in Kauai posted the following suggestions for previewing and walked them through each:

- Look through assigned text.
- Think about what you already know about the topic and what you will be reading.
- Look at titles and headings.
- Look at vocabulary words.
- Look at pictures and captions.
- Read summary, conclusions, questions at the end *FIRST!*
- Be prepared to make predictions and discuss background.

Teacher Read-Alouds in Content Classes

Once the anticipatory set and vocabulary are introduced, *the teacher reads two or so paragraphs to model reading comprehension strategies.* In secondary schools, teachers read aloud to model reading fluency and comprehension skills—*not to read for the students.* There is a strong belief that because students have trouble reading, it is better for the teacher to read to the students. We emphasize this because we have observed teachers read complete novels to their classes! Keeping students from reading only makes them fall further and further behind on their reading skills.

First, the teacher makes *one* of the statements below and then proceeds to model how the statement is done. For instance, a teacher would say:

- I'm going to visualize and think aloud about what I just read.
- I'm going to read chunks I can handle and then summarize.
- I'm going to change the title and subheadings into questions.
- I'm going to make predictions.
- What could that word mean? Let me reread.
- I'm going to stop and reread confusing parts of this sentence.
- I'm going to put a Post-it note after this sentence so I can ask for clarification.
- What kind of test question would the teacher ask from this paragraph?
- How does this relate to the paragraph above?

There are other basic reading (decoding) and reading comprehension skills that can be modeled and taught while doing a teacher read-aloud. Some of the ones ELLs and low-level readers need the most in secondary content classes are listed here along with ways teachers can teach them "on the run" without having to stop and conduct a grammar or phonics lesson.

Modeling Grammar, Spelling, Phonics, and Comprehension Skills During Teacher Read-Alouds

1. *Auditory Blending and Segmenting.* With a difficult word, blend sounds for 2, 3, or 4-phoneme words or break a word into its separate sounds.

2. *Sight Words.* Mention and read words that have irregular spelling or pronunciation.

3. *Vocabulary.* Say the word twice and follow it with a simple definition or a simple sentence.

4. *Cognate Awareness.* Recognize cognates and false cognates, and set up cognate recognition activities.

5. *Spelling.* Say the word, then spell the word aloud as you are reading.

6. *Writing Mechanics.* Mention or emphasize punctuation, sentence structures, grammar, idioms, and metaphors.

7. *Fluency.* Read a sentence without fluency (too slow, too fast, wrong pauses, wrong intonation), then read it again with smoothness, good expression, good rate.

8. *Comprehension Monitoring.* Model comprehension monitoring and "fix-it" strategies. Make a mistake in reading and then go back and fix it.

9. *Predictions.* After reading part of a paragraph, make a prediction.

10. *Questions.* Ask a question after you read a couple of lines.

11. *Answer Questions.* After you ask a question, model answering that question in complete sentences.

12. *Grammar.* Talk about particular sentence structures, tense, punctuation, and contrastive features of Spanish and English (or English and another language when possible).

13. *Word Analysis.* Mention prefixes, suffixes, identifying word parts, and break and assemble compound words.

14. *Summarization.* Read a couple of sentences, then summarize aloud.

15. *Graphic Organizers.* Read a paragraph, then quickly fill out a graphic organizer you have on the board or chart tablet.

16. *Text Related Writing.* Think aloud how you would tackle prewriting, writing, revising, editing, publishing, using vocabulary and patterns from the text you have been reading.

After modeling one or two strategies, the teacher instructs the students to use those same strategies as they conduct their partner reading.

Partner Reading

After the teacher models reading and thinking about reading, partners are assigned a reading portion, which includes rereading what the teacher read aloud. At the beginning of the year, alternating sentences helps students ease into partner reading. This also ensures that partners are paying attention to each other and helps them concentrate on stress and juncture, punctuation (where and how to pause), in other words to read with expression. This form of developing fluency also emphasizes comprehension. After reading a few alternating sentences, students stop and practice the strategy the teacher has assigned (e.g., summarizing). After a few weeks of alternating sentences, partners can move to alternating paragraphs, as long as they continue to be engaged in quality reading and quality interaction. There are several variations students like to use for partner reading. These are some that we have captured:

Partner Reading Option 1

- Partners read the entire page alternating sentences.
- The teacher leads a short discussion of the page to check comprehension.
- Students share a word or words they didn't understand.

Partner Reading Option 2

- Partners read the entire page, alternating sentences.

- Partner A retells what happened or summarizes facts from the first paragraph.

- Partner B retells what happened or summarizes facts in the second paragraph, and so forth until they finish the page.

- Students place Post-it notes on words that they cannot identify or understand.

Before starting partner reading, students need to know the behaviors expected during reading. The section in this chapter on Cooperative Learning suggests ways of setting up effective partnerships and teams.

Partner Reading With Newcomers

Benefits for Mainstream Students. Pairing an ELL or a newcomer ELL with a mainstream student is beneficial for both. It helps the ELL, particularly a newcomer, to have a buddy who can help understand what classroom protocols are like in this country. Mainstream students report they learn a lot more from helping others than they do on their own. This is because they are more cautious about how they read (their fluency), and pay closer attention to what they read, and are able to understand it better because they get to talk through what they just read. Hearing questions from someone who needs explanations for basic word meanings, cultural nuances, and concept formation helps the peer tutor as much as the ELL.

Benefits for Newcomers. Many students will come during the year and need to fit into academic learning as quickly as possible. Some newcomers can do that very well since they have high literacy levels in their own language. Others may need more time, even to figure out what schooling norms are required of them. When a newcomer needs this type of help, placing the student with an established ELL-mainstream partnership works well. When it is time for partner reading, the newcomer sits between the two and listens to each of them read. After a week or so of listening and observing reading protocols and classroom norms, the newcomer begins to feel more comfortable. The next step is to ask the newcomer to shadow read (read after each partner but in a soft voice), or read along with each partner softly. The third step is to ask the student to take turns reading on his own, but still sits between both partners. This way, the student in the middle gets more turns at reading because students are still alternating sentences but the one in the middle gets to read twice as much. This *three-step peer scaffolding process* helps the student "pick up" English quickly and keep up with assignments. If an ESL teacher works with this student some time during the day, that teacher can accelerate vocabulary and reinforce concepts the student has read in the content classes. In the meantime, the mainstream teacher is applying all the steps described throughout this chapter so that there is redundancy of vocabulary usage through the lesson sequence.

Choral Reading in High School?

Students like to get creative with how they read. Choral reading is not just for poetry or theater anymore! A government class decided they would read in unison by teams, one paragraph at a time. After a couple of times, they decided to start practicing their parts before class so they could outperform, outread, the other teams. By practicing prosody in this fashion, government came to life. Some of the students who also had a physical science class together talked the teacher into letting them do the same in the science class. The science teacher took it a bit further and had whole-class rehearsals for reading and pronouncing words such as *elongated, ellipse, perpendicular* so the choral reading would come out smoother. Both teachers reported that choral reading helped all students develop more confidence in using appropriate terminology and reassured ELLs that help was necessary and available even for mainstream students. Choral reading also led students to explore new ways of presenting their unit products more creatively. Some decided to personify the solar system and presented with dialog and movement what they had studied. The government teams also wrote short plays depicting a controversial event that blended history with politics.

Consolidating Knowledge Through Cross-Cutting Strategies

After partner reading, other student-centered and/or teacher-guided activities can be used to consolidate knowledge. We call these activities cross-cutting strategies. Oral, writing, or further reading activities to anchor knowledge can be conducted through Cooperative Learning, journals, logs, and instructional conversations. We call these cross-cutting strategies because they can cut across all content areas and cut across any part of a lesson. These help to build redundancy of concepts and vocabulary—and those pieces of knowledge that will be tested.

Debriefing as a Cross-Cutting Strategy

After about 15 minutes of partner reading, the teacher asks them to pause where they are and begin a discussion of what they "have found so far." This open-ended question signals that students can discuss themes, important details, and confusing lines, question the author or the facts, and clarify concepts and key vocabulary. The teacher usually ends the discussion with another open question, such as "What did you learn?" Besides content, students express lessons learned about working together or things that did not work.

Teachers don't always debrief with the whole class. Sometimes they go from team to team and ask and probe. They conduct instructional conversations where students are welcomed to discuss, question, and think aloud about what they are working on. One history teacher likes to pull 5 chairs together in a corner of the room and calls each team of 4 to come and converse with him for 10 minutes each. These rich conversations are always exciting. Students come prepared because although these are informal conversations, they like to show off their knowledge and even try to trip up the teacher with complex questions. The teacher uses this strategy before tests to get students to talk through the key ideas, details, and inferences from the social studies unit they have been reading and learning. These talk-through conversations help students go beyond answering literal questions about history and to process information at high levels of thought and meet curriculum standards.

Cooperative Learning as a Cross-Cutting Strategy

After reading and discussing ideas with the teacher, the students can work in teams of four to consolidate their knowledge and thinking into a group product. Graphic organizers lend themselves to this type of consolidation. Information learned can also be consolidated into written synopses or summaries. Both products enable students to use the new vocabulary words again, anchoring meaning through utility. They use the words to map out concepts or to write the summaries. They also drill each other on the meaning, spelling, and multiple meanings of the words.

Teachers usually prepare the students to work in teams from the beginning of the year until students learn to work efficiently. Making sure each student has an academic task, not just "one leader" to do all the organizing, thinking, and even the work! They start by assigning simple fun activities so the focus is on learning how to work together. They also present, post, and discuss with students the following norms for working in teams:

- Everyone must contribute ideas
- Everyone must work on all tasks
- Everyone must show respect for peers
- Everyone must learn and master the material

Some teachers like to assign roles at the beginning of the year. Some examples that have explicit roles so that each student is responsible for an academic aspect of the task are:

- Content Connector—discusses connections between new and old information; between instructional objective and information being gathered.
- Architect—responsible for graphing or illustrating meaningful pieces of information.
- Vocabulary Collector—looks for key words and other interesting, unfamiliar, and perhaps relevant words, marks the spot, and shares with the team.
- Seeker—finds interesting, important, or puzzling pieces of information in the text to read aloud to the group.

After students have completed their team product and learned the new vocabulary and concepts, they write in their logs or *exit passes* how this information affects them or their environment or the world. Exit passes are 2" × 3" cards where students write their reflection and hand it to the teacher as they leave the classroom. They make connections to their lives and current events. They can also make connections to other chapters, literature, or discussions they have had in class.

Formulating Questions as a Cross-Cutting Strategy

When adolescents work in teams of four, it is important to give them challenging activities that keep them busy learning minute by minute. Figure 4.2 contains graphic organizers for each level of Bloom's Taxonomy. Each slide has key verbs, question stems, and activities for that particular level. For example, the verbs for the *Knowledge* category, which is basically for recalling or remembering information, are words such as *describe, define, identify, label, recognize.* However, for a higher category such as *Analyzing,* the verbs to be used are words such as *differentiate, distinguish, select.* Questions for this category would be: What conclusions can you draw from . . . ? What is the function of . . . ? The type of products or activities for this would be: Design a . . . Make a flow chart for . . . Analyze . . .

Figure 4.2   Applying Bloom's Taxonomy of Cognitive Process—4

APPLYING BLOOM'S TAXONOMY OF COGNITIVE PROCESS—4			
THINKING PROCESS	*USEFUL VERBS*	*SAMPLE QUESTION STEMS*	*POTENTIAL ACTIVITIES AND PRODUCTS*
A N A L Y S I S	Analyze Distinguish Examine Compare Contrast Investigate Categorize Identify Explain Separate Advertise Subdivide Point out Select Survey Differentiate Classify	What is the function of…? What conclusions can you draw from…? What is the premise? How was this similar to…? What was the underlying theme of…? What do you see as other possible outcomes? Why did …changes occur? Can you compare your… with that presented in…? What must have happened when…? How is … similar to…? What are some of the problems of…? Can you distinguish between…? What was the turning point in the story? What was the problem with…? What were some of the motives behind…?	• Design a questionnaire to gather information. • Make a flow chart to show critical stages. • Write a commercial for a new/familiar product. • Review a book of math and compare to the one we use. • Construct a graph to illustrate selected information. • Construct a jigsaw puzzle. • Analyze a family tree showing relationships. • Write a biography about a person being studied. • Arrange an exhibit and record/list the steps you took.

These frames are given to the students to use throughout the semester. The question stems are useful for constructing questions during partner reading or for cooperative learning activities such as Numbered Heads Together.

In a *Numbered Heads Together* activity, each team writes 2 questions on a given section of the text. One question is from Bloom's knowledge, comprehension, or application category; the other from the analysis, synthesis, or evaluation category. They give these questions and possible answers to the teacher. The teacher uses these questions for a Numbered Heads Together to test the class. In a Numbered Heads Together, the students number off from 1 to 4 in each team; the teacher calls out a question and asks all the teams to put their heads together to discuss the answer and make sure everyone knows the answer; after a couple of minutes, the teacher calls a number, and a student has to stand and respond for the whole team. This strategy is particularly helpful for ELLs because they know they have to be ready to answer as much as the other students and are willing to participate more. The accountability factor also works for the other students because they learn how to help the ELL as well as prepare themselves more accurately.

These questions are sometimes used with the *Tea Party* activity. In a Tea Party students stand either in two concentric circles and face each other, or in two long "conga-type" lines and face each other. The teacher gives them a minute to review, discuss, and memorize each answer. Then she arbitrarily calls on one student to respond. The students then move to the next partner, and another question is discussed. Usually 8 to 10 questions or topics are used for this activity.

When students formulate questions for such competitions, the questions tend to be at higher levels than textbook questions and they also motivate the students. Usually, activities such as these become better assessments of student knowledge than the traditional paper and pencil tests. These activities also save teachers time trying to figure out what questions to ask and how to assess students.

There are many other Cooperative Learning activities that are applicable at any stage of the lesson delivery. The next chapters integrate Cooperative Learning at different intervals and for different purposes.

Graphic Organizers as Cross-Cutting Strategies

Graphic organizers—also called semantic maps, webs, organizers, diagrams, graphs, charts, etc.—are visual representations of knowledge to help students comprehend content (Bromley, Irwin-Devitis, & Modlo, 1995; Echevarria & Graves, 2005). Graphic organizers involve both visual and verbal information; they promote active learning and exercise students' use of language as they listen, think, talk, read, and write. They can also be tools for group interaction between teachers and students and among students. Graphic organizers require the integration of language and thinking to highlight key vocabulary in a visual display of knowledge that facilitates discussion and sharing of ideas and information.

ExC-ELL teachers use graphic organizers to explain concepts for Tier 1, 2, and 3 words. Graphic organizers help ELLs understand grade-level text without changing the meaning or lowering the academic and cognitive level of the content. Graphic organizers help modify difficult texts so content is illustrated in a meaningful way for the students. The four basic patterns used throughout the lesson are:

1. *Hierarchical.* The linear organizer includes a main concept and the levels of subconcepts under it.

2. *Conceptual.* The organizer consists of a central idea with supporting characteristics and/or examples. A Venn diagram is an example of conceptual organizer with two overlapping circles for representing information being compared.

3. *Sequential.* The organizer arranges events in chronological order with a specific beginning and end into chronology, or cause and effect, problem and solution, and process and product.

4. *Cyclical.* The organizer represents a series of events in a circular formation with no beginning or end, just a continuous sequence or successive series of events.

There are many books and Web sites for graphic organizers. By simply typing in "graphic organizers," the Web gave us many many pages of sites (e.g., www.graphic,org; www.smartdraw.com; www .graphic.org), Here is one example we shared with teachers.

Main concept: _____	
Description	**Attribute 1**
Attribute 2	**Attribute 3**

Cooperative Summarizing Activity

Description: Class summaries help students review and remember information. Students can *explain* what they have learned through a summary that focuses on the main concept and three key attributes of that concept. As a subsequent activity, the students can write a report about what they have learned in their team interaction.

Science Theme: _____

Writing as a Cross-Cutting Strategy

Writing intelligently about something is good proof of learning about that subject. Students can meet writing standards by doing their "reports" in a style that fits a writing standard or goal. If one of the goals is descriptive writing, the language arts teacher can meet with the other content teachers and share templates on how to structure the final report. When all content teachers use the same techniques, formats, or templates around the same time, it makes it easier for all students to quickly grasp those formats. Rubrics and ways of evaluating the reports and products should also be consistent across content domains if the final product is to be the same format.

For example, formats for writing position papers can be given, along with information from the Web on opposing views on a government policy, an environmental issue, a way to solve a mathematical problem, or play reviews. Students in teams, pairs or individually can pick sides of the issue and write a position paper defending their position with factual evidence. Students can follow up with debates.

A teacher asked student teams to make a comic book version of a novel they had been reading. The drawing of cartoons had to be accompanied with dialog and intermittent narrative. These are shared with the rest of the class through read-arounds.

Mini lessons are necessary so students can learn to master the writing elements. Nevertheless, mini lessons need to be relevant to ELLs' needs. Some additional features to consider for ELLs:

- Writing lags 1 to 2 levels behind oral language development.
- Syntax, grammar, and spelling errors are the same as in oral language.

This implies that ELLs may need more opportunities for discussions and more models of good writing. Before asking students to write, a teacher can:

- Model brainstorming, drafting, revising, editing, and final publication-ready product.
- Demonstrate and explain what the final written product should look like.
- Explain and display rubrics or criteria for assessing that piece of writing.
- Address different stages of writing development and help students at each stage.

Content teachers can label and share samples of different writing genre, such as:

descriptive	narrative	persuasive
technical manual	history book style	math book style
science book style	chronology	scientific process
web sites	poetry	screen play
short story	mystery novel	marketing plan
reflection journals	learning logs	plain summaries
how to take notes		

Interdisciplinary Products as Cross-Cutting Strategies

The final products can also vary across content domains—some topics lend themselves to dramatizations; others to posters, fliers, newspaper articles; booklets, pamphlets, or technical reports with Web-based information; and a variety of contributions to the community. The biology teacher takes her class to the computer lab at the end of a unit for a week. Her students search the Web for related information in teams, then, pull it together to finalize a team product. One middle school ends a multidisciplinary unit with an Amazing Race where teams compete with a mixture of content, word knowledge, and physical challenges. Everyone enjoys those days, and all students feel accomplished.

Final Debriefing and Student Assessment

Instructional conversations also serve to assess student oracy and comprehension. With the final debriefing through these conversations, the focus turns to the whole chapter, reading segment, or literature piece. Judgments are made about the author's purpose, point of view, quality and clarity of the message, how important this information is, and how it connects to what is happening in the world today. They also do a final sweep of vocabulary terms, and teachers indicate which are key for the final writing product.

Teachers often forget to debrief. They don't leave enough time before the bell rings. One teacher's solution was to set her timer to ring ten minutes before the bell. This way she trained herself and her students to spend that time consolidating knowledge for that period and to gauge what needed to be revisited the next day. After a while, they didn't need the timer. It became inherent, and students automatically stopped to wait for the final instructional conversations with their teacher.

For assessing the overall performance of the students, the ExCELL Observation Protocol can be used. The new format of the EOP uses a Logitech pen to record individual student observations of their oracy and literacy development. When the pen is anchored in its computer cradle a teacher can request graphs of different types to plot the student's progress. The paper versions of the EOP also enable teachers to keep track by storing observations in a student's portfolio. Please see Chapter 9 for oracy and literacy indicators.

"People often confuse *teaching* comprehension skills with *testing* comprehension" (Ivey & Fisher, 2005, p. 13). Content instruction has traditionally called for teachers asking literal questions to test domain knowledge. That is what is called comprehension. If a student did not answer the question, then it was assumed that there was no comprehension. However, that is the old version of comprehension. As content teachers encounter more and more ELLs and low-level readers in their classroom, it will not make sense to expect students to read on their own and comprehend. By the same token, it does not make sense to expect content teachers to become expert reading teachers as they juggle comprehension and domain knowledge.

Therefore, it is imperative that school administrations provide teachers with time to study how to integrate the two. Teachers will need yearlong ongoing support for trying the ideas set forth in this chapter. Teachers who were the most creative and most successful during the year of our first study were given time to get together in their learning communities. They were observed and coached by experts who had conducted or participated in the 10-day training. Their administrators were also trained to observe and support them. Successful students require successful teachers. Teachers who are supported continuously become continuous learners and transmit this to their students.

Table 4.1   Lesson Sequence for Integrating Reading and Oral Language
Development With Subject Matter

	Background Building
Preparing for Reading	• Teacher and students discuss purpose, goal, objectives, I can statements, and background building • Teacher shares rubric or method of grading for this learning objective • Teacher and students discuss method of text organization • Teacher reads aloud to model comprehension strategies, thinking skills, and prosody • Teacher preteaches Tier 1, 2, and 3 vocabulary and engages students to practice each word
	Partner Reading
Prosody	• Students reread the passage the teacher has modeled by alternating sentences as they conduct partner reading • Students read aloud with partners to practice prosody (e.g., reading with expression, intonation, pronunciation, punctuation, pitch, juncture, flow)
Coding Details and Initial Peer Conversations	• Students use Post-it notes or highlighters or simply underline and box: o words pretaught o new words they don't understand o confusing lines o what is most important
Comprehension of Themes and Concepts	• Students make inferences about themes and concepts as soon as they begin reading in pairs. • They continue to check their inferences for accuracy and modifications
	Cross-Cutting Strategies for Consolidating Knowledge
Teacher Debriefs and Class or Small Group Discussions	• The teacher conducts instructional conversations with the whole class or goes from table to table or calls a team to come sit in a comfortable place to discuss any of the following: o themes o most important details o what students found (confusing lines, confusing concepts, questionable elements or facts, author's craft, unknown words, grammatical structures, text organization)

(Continued)

Table 4.1 (Continued)

Cooperative Learning for Comprehension Skills

Students Practice Comprehension Skills Such as Summarizing	• Students reread to the end of the assigned section to summarize/synthesize information through discussions • Students use graphic organizers or cognitive maps to summarize for retell and mastery of content • Students use as many of the key vocabulary words as possible
Connections	• Students reflect on how this information affects them and how they can use it • Students connect information with current events and how this affects their immediate environment or globally • Students connect information with other literature or texts previously read

Student Writing to Anchor Comprehension

Writing Genre	• Students use new vocabulary and concepts through persuasive, informing, or entertaining writing • Students write synopses, essays, narratives, or creative writings (e.g., sonnets, poems, dramatizations, posters, pamphlets, booklets).

Teacher and Students Debrief

Final Debriefing and Assessment	Final Debriefing • Final themes, processes, events, etc. • Author's purpose, facts, formulas, etc. • Judgments of the message's quality, authenticity, clarity, accuracy, relevance, importance to subject matter • Value of vocabulary and content Students' final products are judged on • content • their interpretations • new vocabulary • concepts that have been used Student development of oracy and literacy is documented through the ExC-ELL Observation Protocol and teacher, district, and state assessments.

Summary

✓ Without reading instruction from content area teachers, students get used to surface comprehension.

✓ When students read on their own and answer questions one can never really tell if they are understanding, learning content, or thinking at higher levels beyond literal responses.

✓ With explicit reading instruction from content area teachers students develop critical comprehension, learn vocabulary continually, associate readings with prior knowledge, add new knowledge, interpret facts more accurately, and apply critical thinking to texts.

✓ Student progress on oracy and literacy can be assessed using an observation protocol such as the EOP.

5

Reading, Writing, and Speaking in Mathematics

As teachers of mathematics, we sometimes forget that the words and phrases that are familiar to us are foreign to our students. Students need to master this language if they are to read, understand, and discuss mathematical ideas.

—Thompson & Rubenstein

Thompson and Rubenstein were referring to the issue of language and mathematics learning in mainstream classrooms. They state vocabulary or the fluent use of terminology is a necessary condition for overall mathematics achievement. If the learning of mathematics is highly dependent on its language and the teaching of math vocabulary is crucial, it is doubly so for ELLs.

English language learners in secondary schools should have many opportunities to communicate their mathematical ideas and questions. Talking and writing about their mathematical thinking helps ELLs build word knowledge and oral expression and clarify their thinking. Discussions with the teacher or peers are also useful monitoring tools for teachers. Through listening and recording student conversations and peer problem solving, teachers can monitor individual student progress. Mathematics is no longer viewed as isolated, individualistic, or competitive. Mathematics problems are ideally suited to cooperative group discussions because they have solutions that can be objectively demonstrated. Students can persuade one another by the logic of their arguments. Mathematics problems can often be solved by several different approaches, and students in groups can discuss the merits of different proposed solutions (Robertson, Davidson, & Dees, 1994). For this and several other reasons mentioned throughout this chapter, cooperative learning takes a central place in mathematics instruction.

Teaching and Learning Meaningful Math

The lesson template for ExC-ELL is the same as that described in previous chapters. It begins with stating the learning objectives, background and vocabulary building, and ends with evidence of learning of vocabulary, concepts, and mathematical processes. We will provide an example here.

Reading Comprehension in Math

Planning the lesson. Teachers can begin planning lessons by using a set of questions such as the following to work in the ***text and with the objectives and standards*** they have selected:

Semantic Awareness.

Which Tier 1, 2, and 3 words will I teach?

Which techniques will I use to teach each one?

How can I make sure students interact with each word at least 5 times prior to the lesson? And use the words 7 or more times during the lesson?

Connecting students' prior knowledge with new knowledge.

What are the important mathematical concepts of this lesson? How will I help students link these goals with previous work and with our math standards?

Do the problems or exploration allow for multiple strategies, perspectives, and solutions?

Is the text appropriate, or do I parse it or find another?

What do the students know about this topic? How can I find out?

What type of motivation and props can I use to connect to what we are about to read and learn? How can I make this lesson interesting, accessible, and challenging for students at all levels of mathematical understanding?

What visuals do I use to represent these problems?

Metacognitive Awareness.

Which reading strategies are most appropriate for comprehending the text?

How do I present them in my read-aloud?

Which is the best activity for the students to practice these skills?

How will I debrief what they have learned? What open-ended questions might extend students' thinking?

What questions should I model when introducing the lesson?

Active and engaged reading.

What are the best sections for partner reading?

What strategy should I use for partner reading?

How can I make sure they use the new vocabulary?

Is there a graphic or cognitive organizer they can use?

What follow-up cooperative learning strategy should I use to consolidate knowledge and develop more language skills?

Ample discussions to anchor domain knowledge.

What are my questions for *before reading?*

During reading, where do we stop and debrief?

What are my debriefing questions for the final discussion *after reading?*

What are appropriate sponge activities for teams that finish early or for the next day?

Written product for assessment.

How can I link assessment with this instruction?

What is the best genre for writing up the content they have learned?

What evidence of vocabulary, grammar, critical thinking, and other skills do I want them to exhibit?

What rubrics should I use?

How will I test vocabulary?

Do other types of assessments fit here?

After background building, the teacher reads two or so paragraphs to model reading comprehension strategies. First, the teacher makes one of the statements below and then proceeds to model how to perform the statement. For instance, a teacher would say:

- I'm going to visualize and think aloud about what I just read.
- I'm going to read chunks I can handle and then summarize.
- I'm going to change the title and subheadings into questions.
- I'm going to make predictions before I start to solve the problem.
- What are some possible strategies I might try to solve these problems?
- What has helped teams in the past?
- What could that word mean? Let me reread.
- I'm going to stop and reread confusing parts of this sentence.
- I'm going to put a Post-it note after this sentence so I can ask for clarification.
- What kind of test question would the teacher ask from this paragraph?
- How does this relate to the paragraph above?
- How does this relate to the problem below?

Vocabulary Development for Transmitting Ideas

Math words do not occur in isolation. They are learned in the context of using math concepts during the preteaching of vocabulary before the teacher's read-aloud, explanations on board with students, partner reading, and concept consolidation activities. Thompson and Rubenstein (2000) identify key vocabulary issues that become major hurdles for ELLs and other students. They provide the following examples for teachers because these are easily overlooked and are rarely taught explicitly.

Mathematics and everyday English share some words, but they have distinct meanings:

Number: prime, power, factor

Algebra: origin, function, domain, radical, imaginary

Geometry: volume, leg, right

Statistics/probability: mode, event, combination

Discrete mathematics: tree

Some mathematics words are shared with English and have comparable meanings, but the mathematical meaning is more precise:

Number: divide, equivalent, even, difference

Algebra: continuous, limit, amplitude, slope

Geometry: similar, reflection

Statistics/probability: average

Discrete mathematics: array, edge, and, or

Some words have more than one mathematical meaning:

Number: inverse, round

Algebra: square, range, base, inverse, degree

Geometry: square, round, dimensions, median, base, degree, vertex

Statistics/probability: median, range

Discrete mathematics: sequence or arithmetic sequence, reasoning or circular reasoning.

Some mathematical phrases must be learned and understood in their entirety:

Number: at most, at least

Algebra: one-to-one

Geometry: if-then, if-and-only-if

Statistics/probability: stem-and-leaf

Discrete mathematics: if-then, if-and-only-if

In particular, it is important to highlight to ELLs that some mathematical phonemes are homophones with other everyday words in English. When you are explaining or presenting a lesson, look out for words such as:

sum	some
pair	pear
whole	hole
sine	sign
cosine	cosign
pi	pie
dual	duel
plane	plain
leaf	leave
complement	compliment
graph	graft

Cognates. Mathematics, like other subject areas, are high-cognate languages. English math words are cognates with other languages like Spanish, French, and Italian because they are derived from Latin and Greek roots. That is, they are similar. For instance:

English	*Spanish*
sum	suma
complement	complementar
perpendicular	perpendicular
factor	factor
equation	ecuación
mathematics	matemáticas
algebra	algebra
graph	graf
gram	gram

False cognates or terms to watch out for:

Spanish	*English*
restar	is not *rest,* it means *subtract*
resto	means *remainder* or *"i subtract"*
redondo	round (circle)
redondear	round off

Although most mathematics appears to be a universal language, in English-speaking classrooms a variety of language patterns can occur. Margot Gottlieb (2006) uses the following example to illustrate the many ways a teacher can talk about addition and subtraction:

Addition	*Subtraction*
and	take away
plus	minus
more	less
more than	less than
altogether	diminished by
increased by	are left
sum	remain
in all	fewer
total	from
combine	not as much as
difference	

This means an ELL who has learned only "add" and "subtract" for addition and subtraction may be totally confused 40 out of 41 instances when the teacher is explaining or giving instructions.

If ELLs have studied math in their countries, they will be able to keep up with math much faster than ELLs who have not. This is where differentiation is important. Sometimes, ELLs with rich mathematical backgrounds appear disinterested because they already know the concept. All they need is the language to express what they know. In this instance, differentiated instruction calls for rich vocabulary and oral development.

For ELLs who do not have a mathematical background, additional one-on-one instruction with you or a bilingual instructional resource person will be necessary in order to help the student catch up with both language and content. Simply pairing with another student will not be enough. Pulling the student out of the class with an instructional aide or someone who is not trained in mathematics will not help either. The student needs to be immersed in regular math instruction with quality support through immediate intensive interventions beyond the classroom. Math fluency is like reading fluency. Automaticity of basic skills needs to be achieved before the student can truly comprehend higher math concepts. If the student doesn't know his multiplication tables or understand the intersect between multiplication and division, learning the words will not help him understand. Someone needs to teach him the basics. Just as decoding skills are basic for reading comprehension, basic operations and concepts are the "decoding skills" of math.

Partner Reading

Any textbook or text can be used for partner reading. After the teacher models reading and thinking about reading math, partners are assigned a reading portion, which includes rereading what the teacher read aloud. Each partner reads one sentence at the beginning of the class period. "If a student does not know how to read mathematics out loud, it is difficult to register the mathematics" (Usiskin, 1996, p. 236).

After reading a small section ask the whole class: Turn to your partner and discuss, "What did you notice about the data?"

Next, ask students to continue reading in small chunks. Then stop and:

1. Work together to solve the problems.

2. Decide on a strategy for reading and a strategy for problem solving.

3. Be sure you both agree to the solution before you go to the next problem.

4. Be sure you can both explain how to get your solutions.

5. Be prepared to present problem, process, and solution to the class.

Partner Interview. One way to ensure all students have mastered the concepts, and vocabulary and can present, is to have partners prepare by using the partner interview strategy. Pairs interview each other on the information to be learned, then switch roles. Pairs can then discuss points of weakness and disagreements or agreements, make notes, and role play the interviews again for additional practice.

Teacher and Students
Debrief/Reflect After Partner Reading

Reflection includes mathematical and social aspects of group work. Students need to talk about and hear the strategies, problems, and successes of others. After partner reading and activities, open-ended questions such as these can be asked:

- What strategies did you try? Why?
- What was your solution? Is there another solution that might work?

- What problems did you have? Were you able to solve them? How?
- What are some ways to work that you would recommend to other partners?
- What strategy was particularly helpful to you or your partner?

The debriefing should take no more than 7 minutes. That includes any recommendations you as a teacher might have for your class. Debriefing should, however, be conducted often throughout the period, or after each instructional activity.

Students Work in Teams of Four

There are many cooperative learning strategies for teamwork. All problem solving, explorations, investigations, and creative projects can be done in teams of four. These experiences work best when each student is assigned a specific aspect of a problem to solve or investigate. A note of caution: when roles such as timekeeper, artist, etc., are assigned, the work is typically left to the "problem solver." When a task is evenly distributed among the 4 members, including the ELL, the cooperative process and learning go much more smoothly.

Working in teams gives ELLs more opportunities to "talk mathematics" and teachers opportunities to listen in and "record learning." Teachers can also conduct instructional conversations with teams as they work in teams. They can reinforce correct usage of vocabulary and help students rephrase mathematical ideas, or simply ask questions that elicit the use of key words and concepts.

Teachers like to post or hand out lists of strategies such as the ones below as reminders.

Problem-Solving Strategies

- Act out or use objects
- Use or make a table
- Make an organized list
- Make a picture or diagram
- Use or look for a pattern
- Work backwards
- Use logical reasoning
- Make it simpler
- Brainstorm
- Guess and check

Higher-Order Thinking and Formulating Questions

There are several cooperative learning strategies that can be used with the whole class: Numbered Heads Together, Tea Party, Corners, Line Ups, and Roundtable are some that adapt to many learning tasks and content.

Numbered Heads Together. Each student in a team is numbered from one to four. Then, the teacher posses a question, problem, or issue. Students "put their heads together" and talk this over with the team and make sure all are prepared to respond, especially the ELL. The teacher then calls upon students by number to represent the team. Some teachers give points for correct answers; others just set the context for a challenging game.

Line Ups. Students can be given problems on cards to solve. Then they line up in sequence of results. Or students can line up based on specific categories, such as birthday dates. For this, they line up in bar graph style. For instance all the students born in January stand in a line, all born in February form a second line, and so forth. To find the median birth date and the percentage or fraction of the students born each month, they can huddle in their lines or go back and transfer the information to paper.

Jigsaws. Anything that can be divided into sections can be jigsawed. For instance, a different portion of a text can be given to each team to read, summarize, and prepare to teach to the other teams. Problems at the end of a chapter can also be split up among teams this way. There are different types of jigsaws. There is a simple in-team jigsaw where something is divided into 4 parts and each team member becomes an expert on that part and teaches the others. In another, each team studies a portion and presents or teaches the information to the other teams in a whole-class presentation or by rotating from team to team. A more elaborate jigsaw typically has 4 steps:

1. Task division: A task, passage or text, or a problem is divided into equal parts.

2. Home groups: Each team member is given a topic on which to become an expert.

3. Expert groups: Students who have the same topics meet in expert groups to discuss the topics, master them, and plan how to teach them.

4. Home groups: Students return to their original groups and teach what they learned to their team members.

5. All students take the same test, but individually.

Corners. This is a quick activity that gets student out of their seats and gives them an opportunity to interact with other students since the small groups are randomly selected. All students in the class number off from 1 to 8 or the number that will enable students to stand in different parts of the room in triads or groups of four. The teacher poses a question or problem, and they discuss it. Volunteers share their results with the other groups. As they get ready to go back to their seats, each triad invents a good-bye or 2-line rhyme using terminology they have been discussing.

Roundtable. Each team has only one piece of paper or worksheet and one pencil. One student in the team writes down an answer, says it aloud, and then passes the paper to the person on his right. The process continues until the teacher says stop (usually from 3 to 5 minutes for math). No student is allowed to pass. However, a team can help a student who asks for help. Roundtable can be used with problems such as:

- Find combinations of 2 numbers that add up to 42.
- Give examples of the rule $(a^m)^n = a^{mn}$.
- How many terms in geometry can you list?
- Draw and label as many geometric shapes as you can.

Whatever the strategy used, students will benefit from the interaction. Students who teach other students learn more. ELLs who need help understand better when they have peers to mull over with or to help articulate their thinking.

Final Debriefing and Anchoring of Knowledge

For a final debriefing 5 to 7 minutes before the class ends, teachers usually ask:

What did you learn today?

What made it easier?

What made it difficult?

How can you improve your learning?

How can your team improve for next time?

Student Writing to Anchor Comprehension

Some team writing can be simple compositions prepared as oral recitations to be presented as raps or choral readings. Sometimes students even find ways of making these rhyme, or they borrow lines from other subjects. For instance:

How can we use fractions? Let me count the ways . . .

What are some variable attributes of . . . ? Let me count the ways . . .

What are the differences among the rectangle, square, rhombus, and parallelogram? Let me count the ways . . .

Other team writing. Individual writing can be simple summaries on exit passes or learning logs of what they learned that day. Other times, specific questions can be written on board:

- How many polysemous words did you find today besides *similar?*
- Compare and contrast a rectangle and a rhombus.
- What is the difference between the square of a number and the square root of a number?

As part of a homework writing assignment, ELLs can add visuals or drawings to the definitions or descriptions. These visuals help students see the relationships that they must learn to verbalize. There may be certain processes that are very difficult for ELLs to write about, but they might be able to illustrate them.

When it comes to assessment, performance-based assessments are best. Rubrics will give you a lot of information for individual and team products. These rubrics can be used for you and your students to assess:

- Cooperative learning activities
- Exit passes and learning log entries
- Summaries and reports
- Presentations of math processes

Rubrics are the basis for establishing inter-rater agreement among teachers for performance tasks. Standards-based rubrics can and should be adapted for ELLs. When traditional tests are not logical or practical ways of assessing ELLs, the rubrics or observation protocols become the best way to assess ELLs. For example, in math, an observation protocol might focus on:

1. Does the student use the first language to make meaning?

2. Does the student require more than one explanation?

3. Does the student use pictures to help meaning?

4. Are objects and manipulatives helpful to the student?

5. How often does the student ask peers for help?

6. What type of help does the student ask from peers? From the teacher?

7. Does the student read the problems aloud?

8. Do examples help the student? How?

9. Does the student prefer written or oral directions?

10. Does the student check work done?

Portfolios with an ELL's work help gauge individual progress on a monthly basis. They also serve as evidence for AYP, and as a tool for discussing progress or lack thereof with other teachers and/or the student's parents.

Summary

✓ Math is a language that needs to be pretaught before students can comprehend math texts.

✓ Math problems are ideally suited to Cooperative Learning.

✓ Math is filled with cognates shared between English and Spanish, and bilingual teachers can capitalize on these by explicitly pointing them out.

✓ It is more beneficial for students to learn selected basic concepts and to learn them well than it is to cover many math topics superficially.

6

Reading, Writing, and Speaking in Science

Teaching and Learning Sensible Science

Science can be made terribly exciting or terribly boring! Discovering the excitement in science requires constant use of imagination, curiosity, logic, reasoning, and common sense. Sensible science means enjoying the challenge of the unknown and the unexpected. It is running away with emotion and logic, and running into walls, making wrong turns, and being persistent and relentless in the attempt to reach that goal. These attitudes are enhanced when students, particularly ELLs, experience hands-on science in collaboration with peers. Lazarowitz and Karsenty (1990) find both thinking skills and the use of science process skills are improved when students experience science in cooperative learning activities.

Science is socially constructed through discourse and interactions with others. Many studies have found a consistent relationship between reform practices (hands-on, inquiry, discovery, experiential, project-based, or constructivist) and improved learning, when compared to students in more transmissive or traditional classrooms (Marzano et al., 2001; Anderson, 2002; Wenglinsky, 2002; Stoddart et al., 2002). When a classroom is composed of a variety of language and literacy levels, teaching strategies such as the ones described below help address differentiation. ELLs get to practice more language with hands-on cooperative activities and are cognitively challenged at all times. In cooperative teams, ELLs can learn from what is being displayed in front of them. They learn through experiments as they proceed with their hands-on learning tasks. ELLs need multiple opportunities for using language through problem solving, self-generated elaborations, making affective connections, incorporating graphic and visual representations, pursuing a personal interest through generating and answering questions, and exercising a sense of personal control (O'Malley & Chamot, 1990).

The lesson template for ExC-ELL is the same as that described in previous chapters. It begins with stating the learning objectives, background and vocabulary building, and ends with evidence of learning of vocabulary, concepts, and mathematical processes. We will provide an example here.

Reading Comprehension in Science

Objectives and Standards. There seems to be a consensus among scientists and state standards regarding science. Agreement on the following ideas or themes or salient features of science that should be taught:

- Scientific method and critical testing
- Creativity
- Historical development of scientific knowledge
- Science and questioning
- Diversity of scientific thinking
- Analysis and interpretation of data
- Science and certainty
- Hypothesis and prediction
- Cooperation and collaboration

It is quite evident from this list that it makes sense to teach and learn these attitudes and skills in a social context.

Planning the lesson. Teachers can begin planning lessons by using a set of questions such as the following to work in the *text and the objectives and standards* they have selected:

1. Semantic Awareness.

   Which Tier 1, 2, and 3 words will I teach?

   Which techniques will I use to teach each one?

   How can I make sure students interact with each word at least 5 times prior to the lesson? And use the words 7 or more times during the lesson?

2. Connecting students' prior knowledge with new knowledge.

   What are the important scientific concepts of this lesson? How will I help students link these goals with previous work and with our science standards?

   Do the experiments or exploration allow for multiple strategies, perspectives, and solutions?

   Is the text appropriate, or do I parse it or find another?

   What do the students know about this topic? How can I find out?

   What type of motivation and props can I use to connect to what we are about to read and learn? How can I make this lesson interesting, accessible, and challenging for students at all levels of scientific understanding?

   What visuals do I use to represent these themes?

3. Metacognitive awareness.

   Which reading strategies are most appropriate for comprehending the different types of text the students need to read?

   How should I present them in my read-aloud?

   Which is the best activity for the students to practice these skills?

   How will I debrief what they have learned? What open-ended questions might extend students' thinking?

   What questions should I model when introducing the lesson?

4. Active and engaged reading.

   What are the best sections for partner reading?

   What strategy should I use for partner reading?

How can I make sure they use the new vocabulary?

Is there a graphic or cognitive organizer they can use?

What follow-up cooperative learning strategy should I use to consolidate knowledge and develop more language skills?

5. Ample discussions to anchor domain knowledge.

What are my questions for *before reading?*

During reading, where do we stop and debrief?

What are my debriefing questions for the final discussion *after reading?*

What are appropriate sponge activities for teams that finish early or for the next day?

6. Written product for assessment.

How can I link assessment with this instruction?

What is the best genre for writing up the content they have learned?

What evidence of vocabulary, grammar, critical thinking, and other skills do I want them to exhibit?

What rubrics should I use?

How will I test vocabulary?

What other types of assessments fit here?

After background building, the teacher reads two or so paragraphs to model reading comprehension strategies. First, the teacher makes one of the statements below and then proceeds to model how to enact that statement. For instance, a teacher would say:

- I'm going to visualize and think aloud about what I just read.
- I'm going to read chunks I can handle and then summarize.
- I'm going to change the title and subheadings into questions.
- I'm going to think of a research question(s) before I start the process.
- What are some possible strategies I might try to solve these problems?
- What has helped teams in the past?
- What could that word mean? Let me reread.
- I'm going to stop and reread confusing parts of this sentence.

- I'm going to put a Post-it note after this sentence so I can ask for clarification.
- What kind of test question would the teacher ask from this paragraph?
- How does this relate to our last project?

Vocabulary Development for Transmitting Ideas

Science words do not occur in isolation. They are learned while using concepts during the preteaching of vocabulary, the teacher's read-aloud, students' partner reading and follow-up activities.

Cognates. Mathematics, like other subject areas, are high-cognate languages. English science words are cognates with other languages like Spanish, French and Italian because they are derived from Latin and Greek roots. That is, they are similar. For instance:

Key words are mostly *cognates*:

English	Spanish
hypotheses	hipótesis
observations	observaciones
classification	clasificación
predictions	predicciones
tentative conclusions	concluciones tentativas
experiment	experimento
experimentation	experimentación
investigation	investigación
inferences	inferencias
process	proceso
evaluate	evaluar

False cognates or terms to watch out for:

English	Spanish
pattern	paterno (paternal)

Polysemous Words.

set, table, power, energy, wave, mass, material

Some science words shared with math have different technical meanings in the two disciplines. For instance in math we find:

divide, density, solution, radical, variable, prism, degree, image, radian, simulation, experiment

In particular, it is important to highlight to ELLs that some science phonemes are homophones with other everyday words in English. When you are explaining or presenting a lesson, look out for words such as:

sum	some
facts	fats
axis	exes

Partner Reading

Any textbook or text can be used for partner reading. After the teacher models reading and thinking about reading science, partners are assigned a reading portion, which includes rereading what the teacher read aloud. Each partner reads one sentence initially. Then they move to paragraphs after they learn to read well together.

After reading a small section ask the whole class: Turn to your partner and discuss, "What questions can we generate to study?"

Next, ask students to continue reading in small chunks. Then stop and:

1. Work together to formulate questions.

2. Decide on a strategy for reading and a strategy for formulating questions.

3. Be sure you can both explain your procedure.

4. Be prepared to present inquiry questions and your process to the class.

Partner Interview. One way to ensure all students have mastered the concepts and vocabulary and can present, is to have partners prepare by using the partner interview strategy. Pairs interview each other on the information to be learned, then switch roles. Pairs can then discuss points of weakness and disagreements or agreements, make notes, and role play the interviews again for additional practice.

Debriefing Partner Reading. Reflection includes mathematical and social aspects of group work. Students need to talk about and hear the strategies, problems, and successes of others. After partner reading and activities, open-ended questions such as these can be asked:

- What strategies did you try? Why?
- What was your solution? Is there another solution that might work?
- What problems did you have? Were you able to solve them? How?
- What are some ways to work that you would recommend to other partners?
- What strategy was particularly helpful to you or your partner?

The debriefing should take no more than 7 minutes. That includes any recommendations you as a teacher might have for your class. Debriefing should, however, be conducted often throughout the period, or after each instructional activity.

Setting Up for Student Work in Teams of Four

There are many cooperative learning strategies for teamwork. All problem solving, explorations, investigations, and creative projects can be done in teams of four.

Teambuilding for Science. Teambuilding at the beginning of any group work sets the ground rules for productivity, respect, and inquiry. Students need a fun, simple task to work on initially so the social and productivity skills are practiced and refined through a thorough reflection with the teacher immediately after the teambuilding activity. Usually, a team poster using key vocabulary words (process, solution, element, orbit) is designed by the team. Other artifacts such as name tags or table canisters are designed using the same logo or key words.

Teachers like to post or hand out lists of strategies such as the ones below as reminders.

Problem-Solving Strategies
- Act out or use objects
- Use or make a table
- Make an organized list
- Make a picture or diagram
- Use or look for a pattern
- Work backwards
- Use logical reasoning
- Make it simpler
- Brainstorm
- Guess and check

Higher-Order Thinking and Formulating Questions

There are several cooperative learning strategies that can be used with the whole class: Numbered Heads Together, Tea Party, and Roundtable are some that adapt to many learning tasks and content. A strategy students like because they get to get up and interact with other students is called Corners. In Corners, students stand and cluster in fours around the classroom. They either discuss questions for a test or review what they learned that day.

A creative way of doing Numbered Heads Together in a chemistry class entailed reviewing principles and formulas for density, speed, pressure, and force. After working for a few minutes on a question, the students were asked to put their heads together and select one student to go to another table and share the results.

Final Debriefing and Anchoring of Knowledge.

For a final debriefing 5 to 7 minutes before the class ends, teachers usually ask:

What did you learn today?

What made it easy?

What made it difficult?

How can you improve your learning?

How can your team improve for next time?

Student Writing to Anchor Comprehension

Some team writing can be simple compositions prepared as oral recitations to be presented as raps or choral readings. Sometimes students even find ways of making these rhyme, or they borrow lines from other subjects.

Other team writing. Individual writing can be simple summaries on exit passes or learning logs of what they learned that day. Other times, specific questions can be written on board:

- How many polysemous words did you find today besides *similar?*
- Compare and contrast . . .
- What is the difference between . . .

As part of a homework writing assignment, ELLs can add visuals or drawings to the definitions or descriptions. These visuals help students see the relationships they must learn to verbalize. There may be certain processes that are very difficult for ELLs to write about, but they might be able to illustrate them.

When it comes to assessment, performance-based assessments are best. Rubrics will give you a lot of information for individual and team products. These rubrics can be used for you and your students to assess:

- Cooperative learning activities
- Exit passes and learning log entries
- Summaries and reports
- Presentations of math processes

Rubrics are the basis for establishing inter-rater agreement among teachers for performance tasks. Standards-based rubrics can and should be adapted for ELLs. When traditional tests are not logical or practical ways of assessing ELLs, the rubrics or observation protocols become the best way to assess ELLs. For example, in math, an observation protocol might focus on:

1. Does the student use the first language to make meaning?

2. Does the student require more than one explanation?

3. Does the student use pictures to help meaning?

4. Are objects and manipulatives helpful to the student?

5. How often does the student ask peers for help?

6. What type of help does the student ask from peers? From the teacher?

7. Does the student read the problems aloud?

8. Do examples help the student? How?

9. Does the student prefer written or oral directions?

10. Does the student check work done?

Portfolios with an ELL's work help gauge individual progress on a monthly basis. They also serve as evidence for AYP, and as a tool for discussing progress or lack of with other teachers and/or the student's parents.

Summary

✓ Science can be very exciting or very dull.

✓ Science texts need to be carefully parsed so standards are met.

✓ A variety of texts can be used to learn science. Students need to become familiar with ways to read those texts and write in that genre.

✓ Science is ideally suited to Cooperative Learning.

✓ Scientific concepts and processes are highly dependent on specific vocabulary.

7

Teaching the Art in Language Arts

Language arts create the best opportunities for ELLs to expand their vocabularies and knowledge about the English language, its literature and culture. The American culture is portrayed through its literature. As immigrants are immersed in literature, the social mores, traditions, beliefs, and self-portrayals come to life. Cross-cultural understanding also comes about from reading and discussing authentic literature from other cultures. Students' self-concept and self-esteem are enhanced when literature from their home countries is read, discussed, and appreciated in their classrooms. Social concerns of racism, classism, sexism, environmentalism, and other isms can be discussed in the context of community. Through dialogue, all members of the community review different opinions and interpretations and eventually achieve the ability to interpret text independently, confidently, and insightfully. The lesson template for language arts is the same as that described in previous chapters. It begins with stating the learning objectives, background and vocabulary building, and ends with evidence of learning of vocabulary, concepts, and a rich knowledge base of literature. We will provide an example here.

Planning the Language Arts Lesson

Teachers can begin planning lessons by using a set of questions such as the following to work in the *text and the objectives and standards* they have selected:

1. Semantic Awareness.

   Which Tier 1, 2, and 3 words will I teach?

   Which techniques will I use to teach each one?

   How can I make sure students interact with each word at least 5 times prior to the lesson? And use the words 7 or more times during the lesson?

2. Connecting students' prior knowledge with new knowledge.

   What are the important literature concepts in this lesson? How will I help students link these goals with previous work and with our language arts standards?

   Is the text appropriate, or do I parse it or find another? What do the students know about this theme or author's craft? How can I find out?

   What type of motivation and props can I use to connect to what we are about to read and learn? How can I make this lesson interesting, accessible, and challenging for students at all levels of understanding?

   What visuals or graphic organizers do I use to represent these concepts?

3. Metacognitive awareness.

   Which reading strategies are most appropriate for comprehending this type of text?

   How do I present them in my read-aloud?

   Which is the best activity for the students to practice these skills?

   How will I debrief what they have learned? What open-ended questions might extend students' thinking?

   What questions should I model when introducing the lesson?

4. Active and engaged reading.

   What are the best sections for partner reading?

   What strategy should I use for partner reading? *Reciprocal Teaching? Questioning the Author?* (See boxes on page 98.)

   How can I make sure they use the new vocabulary?

Is there a graphic or cognitive organizer they can use?

What follow-up cooperative learning strategy should I use to consolidate knowledge and develop more language skills?

5. Ample discussions to anchor domain knowledge.

What are my questions before reading?

During reading, where do we stop and debrief?

What are my debriefing questions for the final discussion after reading?

What are appropriate sponge activities for teams that finish early or for the next day?

6. Written product for assessment.

How can I link assessment with this instruction?

What is the best genre for writing up the content they have learned?

What evidence of vocabulary, grammar, critical thinking, and other skills do I want them to exhibit?

What rubrics should I use?

How will I test vocabulary?

Other types of assessments fit here?

Teaching Reading Comprehension Strategies

After background building, the teacher reads two or so paragraphs to model reading comprehension strategies. First, the teacher makes one of the statements below and then proceeds to model the statement that is enacted. For instance, a teacher would say:

- I'm going to visualize and think aloud about what I just read.
- I'm going to read chunks I can handle and then summarize.
- I'm going to change the title and subheadings into questions.
- Let me develop a prediction before I start to read. From this title I predict . . . In the next part I think we will find . . . This will happen next because . . .
- I think I'll use some analogies: It's almost like the time . . . I once saw a flower . . .

- Let me describe my own visual images: I can see those ocean waves . . . This reminds me of a fire blazing . . .
- What are some possible strategies I might try to understand this text?
- How can I find out what that unfamiliar word means? Should I reread the sentence? Does it have a prefix? A suffix? What is the root word?
- I'm going to stop and reread confusing parts of this sentence.
- I'm going to put a Post-it note after this sentence so I can ask for clarification.
- What kind of test question would the teacher ask from this paragraph?
- How does this relate to the paragraph above?
- How does this relate to my predictions?

Teaching Vocabulary Development to Transmit Ideas

Polysemous Words: Some common terms but not for ELLs

Article—a report, an essay that is part of a newspaper, magazine or book; a part of grammar; an object or item, especially one that is part of a group; a section of a legal document.

Body—main section of a piece of writing such as a report or a letter; a human body.

Character—a literary role taken by a human being, a real or personified animal or a personified object; a set of qualities; somebody who has an unusual or eccentric personality; a single letter, number, or symbol.

Novel—a fictional story with characters, setting, and plot; something new, original.

Play—take part in an enjoyable activity; take part in a game; to make a particular shot or stroke in a sporting event; fool around; theatrical production.

Problem—a difficult situation, matter, or person; a question or puzzle; a statement requiring an algebraic, geometric, or other mathematical solution; difficult to discipline or deal with.

Cognates. Language arts, like other subject areas, are high-cognate languages. English words are cognates with other languages like Spanish, French, and Italian because they are derived from Latin and Greek roots. That is, they are similar. For instance:

English	*Spanish*
irony	ironía
rhyme	rima
hero	heroe
fiction	ficción
hyperbole	hipérbola
fable	fabula
comedy	comedia
conflict	conflicto
anecdote	anécdota
autobiography	autobiografía
antagonist	antagonista
metaphor	metáfora
fiction	ficción
protagonist	protagonista
theme	el tema

False cognates or terms to watch out for:

English	*Spanish*
Main character	personaje principal; carácter (personality)

Partner Reading

Any textbook or text can be used for partner reading. After the teacher models reading poetry or narrative, partners are assigned a reading portion, which includes rereading what the teacher read aloud. Each partner reads one sentence at the beginning of the year, then gradually moves to small chunks of text after students learn to read together. After reading the assigned section, the teacher instructs the students to use a reading comprehension strategy such as the ones below:

Partner Reading

- Each partner takes a turn reading.
- Practice active listening as your partner reads.

- Help and encourage reading comprehension.
- Talk about what you read.
- What did you find?
- Got questions?

RECIPROCAL TEACHING Highlights

1. Students predict what they think will happen next before reading each paragraph or segment of text.

2. Students clarify words or text they don't understand by rereading and asking peers for assistance.

3. Students summarize the paragraph or segment of text.

4. Students generate questions after each paragraph or segment of text.

5. A student facilitates the discussion about a paragraph or segment of text.

SOURCE: Palincsar, A. S., & A. L. Brown. (1984). Reciprocal teaching of comprehension-fostering and comprehension monitoring activities. *Cognition and Instruction, 22,* 117–175.

Questioning the Author Highlights

After teachers anticipate problems the students might have with a text and they segment the text where the major ideas occur or where trouble spots might be, they develop queries to supplement the text and get to the quality and depth of meaning.

Initiating queries:

What is the author trying to say here?

What is the author's message?

What is the author talking about?

Follow-up queries:

What does the author mean here?

Does the author explain this clearly?

How does this connect to what the author told us before?

Does the author tell us why?

Why do you think the author tells us this now?

Narrative Inquiries

How do things look for this character now?

How does the author let you know something has changed?

SOURCE: Beck, I. L., M. G. McKeown, R. L. Hamilton, and L. Kucan. (1997). *Questioning the author: An approach for enhancing student engagement with text.* Newark, DE: International Reading Association.

Teacher and Students Debrief/ Reflect After Partner Reading

Reflection includes mathematical and social aspects of group work. Students need to talk about and hear the strategies, problems, and successes of others. After partner reading and activities, open-ended questions such as these can be asked:

- What strategies did you try? Why?
- What was your solution? Is there another solution that might work?
- What problems did you have? Were you able to solve them? How?
- What are some ways to work you would recommend to other partners?
- What strategy was particularly helpful to you or your partner?

The debriefing should take no more than 7 minutes. This time includes any recommendations you as a teacher might have for your class. Debriefing should, however, be conducted often throughout the period, or after each instructional activity.

Students Work in Teams of Four

There are many cooperative learning strategies for teamwork. All problem solving, explorations, investigations, and creative projects can be done in teams of four. Teachers like to post or hand out lists of strategies such as the ones in the box that follows as reminders.

We Analyzed

The Story's

- ☐ Introduction—prior events
- ☐ Characters—round, dynamic, static, flat, protagonist, antagonist
- ☐ Setting—integral, backdrop
- ☐ Conflict—problem
- ☐ Plot—types
- ☐ Variations of plot—foreshadowing, flashback

Author's style

- ☐ Point of view
- ☐ Imagery
- ☐ Figurative language
- ☐ Author's intent

Jigsaws are one of the best methods for studying literature. There are simple jigsaws, where a text is divided among team members for in-depth study and then teaching to other members. There are also more elaborate expert jigsaws where a whole team becomes expert in a given theme (multiplicity, duplicity, utopia), poem, or a section of a novel. For example, a tenth-grade teacher formed teams of three. She gave each team strips from a Shakespearean sonnet to put together, read, and explain to the class. The students loved the challenge and worked very efficiently in a brief period of time because the teams were small.

Higher-Order Thinking and Formulating Questions

Students can use the Bloom boxes to formulate questions. You can select the type of questions they need to practice. Maybe one week they can be all from the Synthesis box; another week, you can ask them to write one from each Bloom level. Variation is good because it keeps students engaged. The teams can formulate anywhere from 2 to 6 questions. Quality is more important than quantity.

After writing the questions by team, they should share them with the class. There are several cooperative learning strategies that can be used with the whole class: *Corners, Numbered Heads*

Figure 7.1   Applying Bloom's Taxonomy of Cognitive Process—6

APPLYING BLOOM'S TAXONOMY OF COGNITIVE PROCESS—6			
THINKING PROCESS	USEFUL VERBS	SAMPLE QUESTIONS STEMS	POTENTIAL ACTIVITIES AND PRODUCTS
E V A L U A T I O N	Judge Select Choose Decide Justify Debate Verify Argue Recommend Discuss Determine Prioritize Access Rate	Is there a better solution to…? Judge the value of… Defend your position about… Do you think…is a good or bad thing? Explain. How would you have handled…? What changes to…would you recommend? Why? Do you believe…? Are you a …person? Why? How would you feel if…? How effective are…? What do you think about…?	• Prepare a list of criteria to judge…show. Indicate priority and ratings. • Conduct a debate about an area of special interest. • Make a booklet about 5 rules you value. • Form a panel to discuss a topic. State criteria. • Write a letter to…advising changes needed. • Prepare arguments to present your view about…

Together, and *Tea Party* are most appropriate for sharing questions or challenging other teams to answer their questions. Using *Corners*, one teacher asks students to number off from one to four and then sends them to stand together in each corner of the room to get others' opinions about their questions. One favorite in all classrooms is *Numbered Heads Together* because it ensures even ELLs can participate and feel successful. It gives all students an opportunity to master material and feel confident about standing up and delivering when their number is called. A twelfth-grade teacher uses a *Congo Line* (variation of the Tea Party), where students form a long line facing each other and use their questions to drill each other on characteristics and interpretations of a novel or play the day before a test. Both the Tea Party and Numbered Heads Together steps are described in Chapter 4.

Final Debriefing and Anchoring of Knowledge

For a final debriefing 5 to 7 minutes before the end of class, teachers usually ask:

What did you learn today?

What made it easier?

What made it difficult?

How can you improve your learning?

How can your team improve for next time?

Student Writing to Anchor Comprehension

Some team writing can be simple compositions prepared as oral recitations to be presented as poems, raps or choral readings.

Other Team Writing

Individual writing can be simple summaries on exit passes or learning logs of what they learned that day. Other times, specific questions can be written on board:

How many polysemous words did you find today besides *similar?*

Compare and contrast these characters, plots, problems . . .

What is the difference between foreshadowing and flashback?

Broad questions can be used with team ***Roundtable*** activities:

- How many key vocabulary words can you remember from this chapter?
- List character of this novel.
- Use key words to describe this character.
- List the elements of realistic fiction.

In a Roundtable activity, the teacher gives the following instructions:

- Clear your desks.
- Use only one paper and pencil per team.
- Each student writes one answer and passes the paper to the right.
- Everyone must write an answer.
- Continue this process until the teacher calls time out.
- The team that has the most correct responses wins.

As part of a homework writing assignment, ELLs can map out a story line, draw a protagonist's personality or changes, add visuals or drawings to the definitions or descriptions. These visuals help students see the relationships they must learn to verbalize. There may be certain processes that are very difficult for ELLs to write about, but they might be able to illustrate them.

One way to help ELLs and other reluctant writers start writing is to utilize team writing. After reading a literature piece, teams can do story-related writing by using the same format or author's craft to write a similar piece. For instance, after reading *Dreamspeaker*, the team can use a **WriteAround** technique to compose their own piece about cultural intolerance; or after reading *The Color Purple*, they can write about personal emancipation. The WriteAround is the same as the Roundtable except that all students have a piece of paper and pencil, and more time is allocated for writing.

When it comes to assessment, performance-based assessments are best. Rubrics will give you a lot of information for individual and team products. These rubrics can be used for you and your students to assess:

- Cooperative learning activities
- Exit passes and learning log entries
- Summaries and reports
- Presentations of math processes

Rubrics are the basis for establishing inter-rater agreement among teachers for performance tasks. Standards-based rubrics can and should be adapted for ELLs. When traditional tests are not logical nor practical ways of assessing ELLs, the rubrics or observation protocols become the best way to assess ELLs. For example, an observation protocol might focus on:

1. Does the student use the first language to make meaning?

2. Does the student require more than one explanation?

3. Does the student use pictures to help meaning?

4. Are objects and manipulatives helpful to the student?

5. How often does the student ask peers for help?

6. What type of help does the student ask from peers? From the teacher?

7. Does the student read aloud?

8. Do examples help the student? How?

9. Does the student prefer written or oral directions?

10. Does the student check work done?

Portfolios with ELLs' work help gauge individual progress on a monthly basis. They also serve as evidence for AYP, and as a tool to discuss progress or lack thereof with other teachers and/or the student's parents.

Summary

✓ Although language arts implies teaching reading, it may not be so as frequently or intensely as necessary for some students.

✓ Vocabulary instruction must also be part of a comprehensive language/literacy curriculum.

✓ ELLs benefit from ample discussion with peers and teachers in order to reach a depth of comprehension of most literature selections.

✓ Reading aloud with peers or teachers help ELLs become aware of what is meant by fluency. They need role models. It is difficult to develop fluency when all ELLs are grouped together for language arts/ESL.

✓ Writing helps ELLs acquire a better sense of writer's craft.

✓ There are many cognates shared by Spanish and English in language arts.

✓ Methods such as Reciprocal Teaching and Questioning the Author help ELLs organize their thinking and language, no matter how limited, to express those thoughts.

8

A Vignette of Social Studies Teachers Developing and Implementing a Lesson

Ways of teaching social studies have not received as much attention. Public presentations to the National Research Council's Committee on Teacher Preparation have reiterated the fact that there is no report out in the field such as that produced by the National Reading Panel to offer research and practice guidelines. Since research-based models for mainstream students are scarce, we can assume that models for teaching social studies for ELLs are scant. Nevertheless, we are capturing lessons that teachers have developed and that have achieved positive student results in terms of language and reading development. The lesson described below by Dr. Liliana Minaya-Rowe, during one of her classroom ethnographies, provides an example of what social studies and ELL teachers do.

Lesson Planning

Trade and Bartering Skits

Objective: Identify how Phoenicians used coin money.

Word and Theme of the Day: Phoenicia

Setting the Target: Social studies teacher and ESL teacher meet to examine the chapter on trade and bartering of the current social studies sixth-grade textbook and compare the contents to the state and district's social studies standards and English language proficiency standards. They plan the following activities:

A. They segment and parse the text. They select those pages from the textbook to use during this week, and decide how much of the content on trade and bartering they want students to learn.

B. They try to make sure that the amount of material to be covered can build a strong foundation for the topic lesson and unit.

C. They select the number of vocabulary words needed from Tiers 2 and 3 and write them on the board.

D. They select the cognates: economy-economía, colony-colonia, cultural-cultural, diffusion-difusión, Lydians-Lidios, Phoenicians-Fenicios. They are aware and also discuss that the students might be familiar with the words but may not know the specific concept—e.g., colonia-colony.

E. They identify the content concepts and the words that they would like their students to learn today.

F. They identify visuals, graphic organizers, role plays, and other activities for building background knowledge.

G. They examine the myriad activities, strategies, and tools they can use to teach vocabulary. They select activities for:

Building background

Remembering what is important (working memory)

Recognizing the word and its meaning with the activity

Preteaching Vocabulary

Tier 1 and 2 words written on the board: *coin, societies, ancient, bronze, statue, tool, dye, worth, merchant, doubtfulness.*

Tier 3 words written on the board: *barter, economy, trade, colony, cultural, diffusion, Lydians, Phoenicians, goods.*

The social studies teacher reads each word, and the students repeat it.

Teacher provides definition for each word with examples.

Teacher asks students to say the word three times.

ESL teacher involves the students in activities to use each word:

> Semantic organizers—Students work in pairs to generate a sentence using the key word.

> Roundtable—Students work in groups writing answers using the target word.

The social studies teacher reads the words once more, and the students repeat them.

Duration of activity: about 7 minutes.

Reading Instruction—Engagement with Text

Before Reading Activities

Activity instructions:

- ESL teacher reads the first section out loud. She reads the first paragraph and models. She goes back and rereads the word so that students use the same decoding strategy.
- Duration of the activity = 3 minutes.

During Reading

Social studies teacher does a think-aloud for metacognitive strategies. She organizes thinking and the social studies lesson concepts via cognitive, vocabulary and content maps, graphic organizers and outlines. She models both reading and maps simultaneously.

Partner reading: Partners read a page in unison. ESL teacher leads a short discussion of the page to check for comprehension and has the students explain the meaning of the target words.

Social studies teacher poses Bloom-type questions with different levels of questioning strategies.

- Duration of activity = 10 minutes.

Consolidation and Debriefing

On a transparency: Trade was an important part of the Phoenician and Lydian societies. The Lydians introduced coin money, which made trading easier.

Both social studies and ESL teachers facilitate the activity. They announce that the activity will continue the following class:

Instructions to Students

Step 1: Coin making

- You and your partner are going to make 10 coins.
- The coins should be small (not much bigger than beans) and should be of equal weight.
- You can design the coins as you like.
- Suggestion: You can use the table on page 111 of your social studies book, or use items that you think were important to these ancient societies.
- Duration = 5 minutes.

Step 2: Determine the value of your coins

- How much will the following items cost? A small vial of purple, a goat, a book, a small sailboat, a bronze statue, a wheeled cart, a tool such as a hammer.
- List the number of coins for each item.
- Suggestion: Develop a small table to present how much each item costs.
- Duration = 5 minutes.

Step 3: Create a skit

- You are going to write a skit with your partner using the scenario below.
- After writing it, you need to practice reading it.
- You need to perform your skit in front of the class.
- Your performance will be graded by your peers.
- While your peers are performing, you will be grading their performances.
- Activity starts during this class and continues as homework for the next class.

Scenario

- Partner A: You are a Lydian and have a bag of coins. You have traveled to Phoenicia because you need to buy 3 items, including a vial of purple dye for your king. You must persuade the merchant to accept your coins so that you can buy things. You need to convince him or her that your coins are worth something.
- Partner B: You are a Phoenician merchant and have many things to sell, including purple dye. You have seen the Lydian coins before and don't know if you should accept them. You usually barter and exchange goods for other goods. You need to express your doubtfulness to the merchant.
- If you want to use props, you and your partner may create props as homework.

Step 4: Perform Your Skit

- *Grading criteria:* Students develop criteria to rate/assess their classmate's performance and to be rated. They propose the following criteria:
  - o Takes skit seriously
  - o Seems prepared
  - o Followed the instructions

  Students rate their classmates as Excellent (3), Good (2), and Poor (1)

  Duration = 20 minutes

Debriefing

The social studies teacher briefly discussed the activity with the students and what they had learned from it. Students said they

- ✓ Talked to their peers (practiced oral language),
- ✓ Asked questions,
- ✓ Learned about the Phoenician's ways of life (content),
- ✓ Solved problems, and
- ✓ Had to memorize the skit (memorization skills).

Duration = 5 minutes

Assessment

⇒ Closing WriteAround Activity to summarize what was learned today and the class before.

⇒ Social studies teacher gives the following instructions:

- Each team has one piece of paper and a pen.
- Social studies teacher gives a sentence starter:

"Today I learned. . ." She instructs the students to finish that sentence and pass it to the right in their group. Invented spelling was accepted.

- The team writes small paragraphs.
- Duration = 3 minutes.

⇒ ESL teacher gives the following instructions:

1. Finish the sentence you are writing, and then let's do the read-around.

2. Read the paper you are holding to your team members.

3. Select the one you like the best.

4. Write a conclusion.

5. Share your team piece with everyone.

- Groups read their pieces to the entire class.

9

Setting the Context for Teachers to Succeed

Professional Development for Teaching Content Area Literacy to ELLs

A Framework for the Preparation of Teachers of ELLs to Teach Reading and Content in the Secondary Schools

The purpose of this chapter is to share the findings from the ExC-ELL research on ways to enhance professional development programs. It is the hope of the author that this framework will assist school districts in the design and implementation of quality professional development programs centered on teaching literacy or biliteracy through social studies, science, math, and/or language arts domains.

Why Focus on Quality Teachers for Reading in the Content Areas?

The National Reading Panel (NRP; 2000) and the Reading Next researchers and policy makers were highly concerned with teacher education for reading. The NRP found preservice education focuses on changing teacher behavior without a concomitant focus on the outcomes of students who are eventually instructed by those teachers. This emphasis is also apparent in the field with the onslaught of "reading models" where the developers are quick to attribute student outcomes to their intervention and not the teachers. Although reading instruction involves four interacting factors: students, tasks, materials, and teachers, the NRP found research has rarely focused on teachers, instead emphasizing students, materials, and tasks. Therefore, teacher education and its impact on the teachers' and their students' learning has been largely ignored.

As indicated in the previous chapter, there is a general scientific consensus among researchers and comprehensive research review panels that certain components are necessary for teaching basic reading skills (Learning First Alliance, 2000; National Reading Panel, 2000; Pacific Resources for Education and Learning, 2002; Slavin & Cheung, in press; Snow, Burns & Griffin, 1998). This research has been incorporated into the Reading First initiative that directs attention to reading in the primary grades. However, recent efforts are looking at reading in secondary schools. In *Reading Next: A Vision for Action and Research in Middle and High School Literacy* (Biancarosa & Snow, 2004) attention was finally given to comprehension, learning while reading, reading content areas, and reading in the service of secondary or higher education, of employability, of citizenship.

> Educators must figure out how to ensure that every student gets beyond the basic literacy skills of the early elementary grades, to the more challenging and more rewarding literacy of the middle and secondary school years. Inevitably, this will require, for many of those students, teaching them new literacy skills: how to read purposefully, select materials that are of interest, learn from those materials, figure out the meanings of unfamiliar words, integrate new information with information previously known, resolve conflicting content in different texts, differentiate fact from opinion, and recognize the perspective of the writer—in short, they must be taught how to comprehend (p. 1).

Through the specific recommendation from the Carnegie Corporation of New York, part of the ExC-ELL project was to study and "figure out" how to design staff development programs for middle and high school teachers of language arts, English as a second language, social studies, science, and math.

The Process of Staff Development

The process for professional development itself must be based on research. Making sense of experience and transforming professional knowledge into teaching habits requires time and a variety of professional activities (Learning First Alliance, 2000). Recognizing the link between professional development and successful educational change (Darling-Hammond & McLaughlin, 1995; Lieberman, 1995), and results-driven education (Sparks & Hirsh, 1997), quality teacher training has to be offered to teachers of ELLs. For teachers to learn a new behavior and effectively transfer it to the classroom, several steps need to be included in the design.

Teachers need theory, research, modeling or demonstrations of instructional methods, coaching during practice, and feedback in order to integrate instructional practices into their active teaching repertoire (Joyce & Showers, 1988). For example, teachers would need presentations on cutting-edge theory and research on reading/literacy; experts to model effective strategies for building word knowledge, comprehension, and writing for teaching English language learners; and time to practice and exchange ideas with peers after each segment or activity of the presentation (Calderón, Minaya-Rowe, & Carreón, 2006). Adult learners need to inquire, reflect, and respond to new ideas if they are to embrace them. Therefore, a teacher-oriented program would provide low-risk practice sessions in a workshop setting where teachers can practice teaching strategies in small teams. It is also important to distill research on a given topic into a dozen or so principles, after teachers have read the research. Workshop presenters could provide opportunities for reading and teacher reflection through cooperative learning activities. Presenters should also include as part of their workshop, explanations and demonstrations of peer coaching practices that promote the transfer of new teaching skills into the classroom (Calderón, 1994; Joyce & Showers, 1988).

When Bruce Joyce and Beverly Showers worked with our Multidistrict Trainer of Trainers Institutes years ago, they used the matrix below to illustrate the outcomes of each component of training. When

Figure 9.1   Staff Development Components and Learning
Communities

Importance of TLCs

Types of Training Components	Level of Knowledge		Transfer one year later	
			Teacher Use	Student Effect Size
Theory and Lecture	80%	5%	5%	0.01
Modeling and Demos	90–95%	50%	5%	0.03
Practice and Feedback	95–100%	80–90%	5%	0.39
Coaching and TLC's	95–100%	98–100%	75–95%	1.68

lectures or theory is the only component presented to teachers, there is only minimal transfer into the classroom. At the end of the school year, we predict approximately 5% of the teachers will be using the new strategies. This 5 or so percent comprises teachers who figured out how to implement that research. Unfortunately, such a small number of teachers will have minimal impact on student outcomes. Sometimes other teachers set out to discourage the "brave pioneers." In many cases, it is only the ESL teacher who attends an inservice to learn about ELLs. On the other hand, when theory, demonstrations, practice, feedback and coaching/collegial activities are integrated into a comprehensive staff development program, both teacher transfer into the classroom and positive student outcomes are the result. Concomitantly, the more teachers that attend the inservice, the more powerful the student results.

Staff Development Models and Outcomes

Another way of looking at the impact of a training design is to consider the differences between these two models:

Model A—Consists of (1) a 5- to 10-day workshop on a new reading program conducted during the summer or at the beginning of the school year without follow-up support for teachers;

Model B—Consists of (1) a 5- to 10-day workshop with (2) follow-up support for teachers, and (3) rigorous measures to determine training, teacher, and student outcomes.

When we compare these two designs we see teachers remain at an initial level of knowledge and instructional skill without impact on students for the first design. In the second design, there is structured follow-up from an inservice through school-based Teachers Learning Communities and appropriate measures. In model B, teachers can reach an expert level in even one year. What's more, the impact on their students becomes significant.

Figure 9.2   Expected Teacher and Student Results

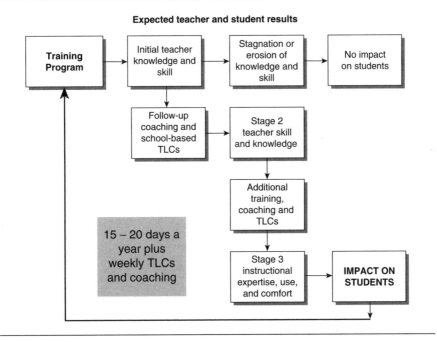

A backwards-planning approach to staff development designs enables one to focus on the student outcomes a school desires.

For instance, if the students need intensive quality instruction on vocabulary development for everyday communication and subject matter learning, the design begins

Results-driven education and teacher-focused professional development needs to begin by determining the things ELLs need to know and be able to do; then, working backwards to the knowledge, skills, and attitudes required of educators if those student outcomes are to be realized.

with that vocabulary development as the desired outcome. In order to measure such an outcome, the teachers and students benefiting from a vocabulary development staff development treatment need to be measured against a nontreatment group. The teachers' level of knowledge about vocabulary, the quality of their instructional repertoire for teaching vocabulary, the frequency and use of those strategies, and the way they adapt them to ELLs and other students, are all important to measure. This is what we refer to as *transfer from training into the classroom*—how well, how often, and how effectively teachers use the new strategies learned at any inservice in their own classrooms.

Figure 9.3   Relationship Between Training, Teacher and Student Outcomes

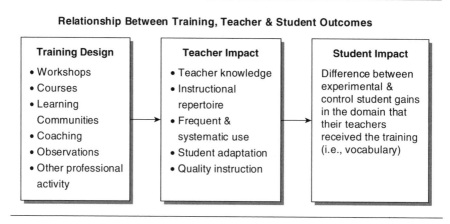

Continuing with the vocabulary example, as the decisions are made for the staff development design, measures and instrumentation for data collection must also be determined. At the student level, measures should be connected to the staff development focus as much as possible. For a vocabulary intervention, pre- and posttests of vocabulary in each content area can be used for both experimental and control student cohorts. The vocabulary subtest of a standardized test such as the Woodcock-Johnson can also be used to measure and compare. If, as we know, vocabulary correlates with reading comprehension, then a test of reading comprehension can also be used. Student writing samples collected on a monthly basis are also good indicators of application, depth, and breadth of word knowledge.

Students learn what teachers teach, and then some. Classroom observation instruments such as the EOP can help supervisors, coaches, and the teachers themselves gauge the progress of quality instruction. Video analysis, analysis of student work, and exchanges in TLCs are indicators of teachers' progress. The EOP also shows the creative contributions of each teacher.

Teachers learn what teacher trainers teach, and then some. Ways of measuring the effect of the staff development intervention are usually self-reporting evaluations, which basically tell us about the climate in the room, the food, and how they felt about a trainer. Rigor needs to be built into the training evaluation in order to anticipate strong or weak outcomes, and to redesign the training based on those weaknesses. Otherwise, we are shortchanging our teachers.

Some key indicators in the form of a question can be:

1. Is the information being presented at the cutting edge of research-based knowledge? This is particularly important when it comes to ELL instruction, since most presenters are still espousing theories that have never been proven by research.

2. Is the research accompanied with practical instructional strategies and techniques, or do teachers have to figure these out on their own?

3. What is the teacher interaction during those workshops? Are they excited as they participate in the demonstrations?

4. Do their questions reflect interest in application? Do their comments reflect excitement about trying them out and how applicable it all is to their ELLs and their other students?

5. Finally, is all this relevant to their students? Is it grade-level appropriate? Is it content-appropriate?

Micro-level indicators for classroom implementation of level of impact can include:

1. Do students learn 5 to 10 new words during a class period and use them in retells, conversations, writing, and comprehension tests?

Figure 9.4   Example: Workshops on Vocabulary

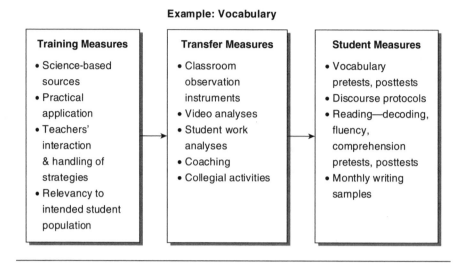

Example: Vocabulary

Training Measures	Transfer Measures	Student Measures
• Science-based sources • Practical application • Teachers' interaction & handling of strategies • Relevancy to intended student population	• Classroom observation instruments • Video analyses • Student work analyses • Coaching • Collegial activities	• Vocabulary pretests, posttests • Discourse protocols • Reading—decoding, fluency, comprehension pretests, posttests • Monthly writing samples

2. Can teachers cite sources and explain the research-based instructional strategies they are using?

3. Does each teacher use a variety of effective strategies for teaching vocabulary?

4. Does the teacher invite other teachers to come and observe her or him teach for feedback and for sharing strategies?

5. Do the training sessions focus on research and demonstrate many strategies for vocabulary development and how they apply to ELLs?

Duration of Training

A comprehensive staff development design would begin with an initial 5- to 10-day workshop followed by another 10 days of lesson integration and parsing of texts. When school starts, teacher practice in the classroom is accompanied with weekly 30-minute discussions with teacher colleagues in Teachers Learning Communities (TLCs). In addition to the collegial learning at the school site, two or three additional days of inservice will be needed as refreshers and for building additional concepts, skills, and creative application. Some teachers will progress more rapidly with the integration of new learning into their teaching styles and student diversity. These quick learners can become

Figure 9.5   Some Indicators of Success

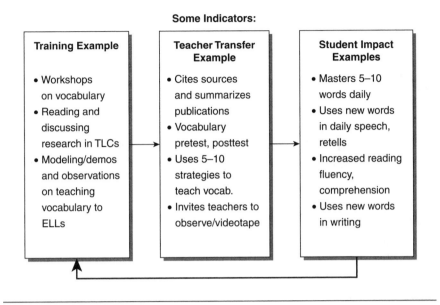

peer coaches or mentors of others who need more confidence or technical assistance. Some teachers need to observe a strategy 5 or 6 times before they feel comfortable applying it; others need 20 observations. A one-size workshop does not fit all. If we are to individualize student learning, we must begin by individualizing teacher learning. Options we can offer teachers for their own professional growth are:

* Study groups

* Lesson development

* Peer coaching

* Action research (individual or with colleagues)

* Teacher portfolios

* Cultural histories/autobiography

* Train other teachers

Weekly Collegial Study

According to Guskey (1998), Joyce & Showers (1988), and others, collegial activity is key for continuous learning on the job. Even after an inservice training, seasoned teachers need time to reflect and adapt new learning into their teaching. We can forecast the level of transfer based on the type of collegial activities teachers conduct on a weekly basis. We can easily predict that without collegial activity, teachers will begin to feel uncomfortable with an innovation after four weeks, and usually stop using the new instructional behaviors shortly thereafter. For this reason, it is critically important to build collegial skills and the mind-set of continuous learning with peers before the inservice ends. Otherwise, the teachers will go back to their old familiar ways of teaching before the end of the school year.

As part of the inservice on literacy for ELLs, teachers need to learn how to set up and run their own TLCs. The studies of TLCs in schools have documented collegial activities of teachers as follows: to model new strategies for each other; solve problems of student adaptation; share their creativity through concrete products (lessons, curriculum, tests, etc.); analyze and evaluate student work regularly; provide ongoing peer support, responsiveness, and assistance to all teachers; share and discuss issues of classroom implementation, transfer from training, impact of teacher on student behavior and learning; share ideas for new lessons or next steps; and schedule peer observations and coaching (Calderón, 1994, 1999, 2000; Calderón & Minaya-Rowe, 2003). Results from the students' pretests and posttests in the ExC-ELL project correlated with the level of TLC activities of teachers.

When well implemented, TLCs can be places and spaces where teachers collaboratively examine, profoundly question, develop, experiment, implement, evaluate, and create exciting change. TLCs are opportunities for teachers to coconstruct meaning to their craft and do whatever is necessary to help each other implement an innovation with fidelity. When studies are being conducted in their classrooms, teachers become coresearchers and eagerly contribute to the research and development of new programs. Their creative talents emerge as a new type of professional environment is established where they are respected for their expertise.

Teachers' Learning Communities (TLCs) are places and spaces where teachers can collaboratively examine, question, develop, experiment, implement, evaluate, and create change.

However, our studies (Calderón, 1984; Calderón et al., 2005; Calderón, Minaya-Rowe, & Durán, 2005) have also documented the need to provide teachers with theory and practice on how to work in collegial teams. Because collegiality is difficult for many adults, the concept of collegiality needs to be established and practiced during all inservice workshops. It is also important to recognize that teachers add analytical, creative, and practical learning to their teaching and assessment methods. The tables below list ways teachers have used TLCs to further their and their peers' learning. Perhaps the most exciting side effect of TLCs is the TLC teachers receive from one another during critical times of change and difficulty, such as dealing with new assessments and NCLB regulations.

Teachers learn how to analyze student products, interpret student data, and discuss implications for instructional improvement. Interpreting standardized test results can be most cumbersome and complex if it is done in collaboration with others who have the same interests.

What do teachers do in TLCs?

- Analyze student performance data
- Reevaluate ELL outcomes every 2 weeks
- Work on instructional improvement
- Study student writing and rubrics used
- Share lessons with the 10 components
- Ask for suggestions on strategies

Teachers are presented at the workshop with ideas for the first few TLC sessions such as the ones on this page, but eventually, they themselves invent and design ways that are more efficient and beneficial for them.

Summer Curriculum Institutes

A well-skilled worker is nothing without his or her proper tools. Teachers need carefully crafted lesson plans and yearlong curricula to accomplish their tasks. As part of a comprehensive staff development, teachers will need 2 to 4 weeks in the summer to integrate new reading strategies into their lessons, curriculum standards, and assessments. It is foolish to require teachers to do all this during the year as they are teaching and attempting to learn something new.

Administrator Training for Teacher Support

Principals, curriculum coordinators, mentors, and other support personnel need to be well equipped to assist teachers in this difficult phase. They need to be required to attend the workshops, and to attend one where "teacher support mechanisms" is the topic. A similarly useful session to attend would be "helping teachers recognize and capitalize on their strengths." Forming a successful teacher development program will require building communities of practice where teachers, administrators, and students are learning all the time. As additional research on reading continues to emerge, pedagogy must adapt and readapt. As teachers are better prepared to teach reading, particularly to ELLs, students' chances for learning to read will significantly increase.

> The administrator's job is to provide leadership, resources, and time for inservice training and TLCs for job-embedded learning. No one can expect teachers to accomplish all this on their own time!!!

Allocating time for staff development and time for TLCs is the first step toward success. The next step is to make sure teachers receive implementation visits from their administrators and coaches for technical support and troubleshooting throughout the year. Yet sustaining continuous learning and collegial activities will need a well-defined plan of implementation that needs to be revisited by teachers, coaches, and administrators 3 or 4 times a year. We have collected ideas from successful implementations from different parts of the country, which are synthesized below.

Sustaining Quality TLCs

- TLC activities need to be structured by specific agendas generated by teachers—the agenda should be flexible enough to allow teachers to meet their own emergent needs.
- TLC activities need to be brief—5 minutes for sharing successes, 5 minutes for problem solving, 10 minutes for instructional demos, 10 minutes for analyzing student work, 5 minutes for celebration.
- TLC activities need to be scheduled—as part of the school's calendar, and time has to be allocated during the workday.

Implications for Implementation: Accountability and Quality

With poor English language learner outcomes and more emphasis on accountability by state and national policymakers, transforming teaching practices has to go hand in hand with transforming professional development practices. Hard-nosed empirical studies and evaluation of staff development programs has to be applied each time a workshop, an inservice, or the implementation of a new program is being contemplated. We do not have a culture of rigorous professional development yet, much less an overabundance of evidence for what defines a high-quality teacher and what practices represent effective teaching for ELLs. As the National Literacy Panel for Language Minority Children and Youth and the Carnegie Foundation Panel conclude their findings, we can begin to make sure all teacher training attempts are guided by evidence. For now, we have this empirically tested model to begin to guide us.

Summary

✓ Any professional development program must be comprehensive and systematic.

✓ All teachers in secondary schools benefit from professional development programs focusing on reading in the content areas.

✓ Teachers' Learning Communities (TLCs) are just as important as inservices, and sustain what teachers learn at an inservice.

✓ TLCs must be allocated quality time during the school week.

✓ TLCs need to be carefully crafted.

✓ There's a direct correlation between the quality and intensity of a professional development program and student outcomes.

10

New Directions in Coaching and Classroom Observation

So it follows naturally that literacy coaching—a form of highly targeted professional development—is a particularly potent vehicle for improving reading skills

—Standards for Middle School and
High School Coaches

M ost secondary schools now have literacy coaches, mainly due to the emphasis on literacy (Biancarosa & Snow, 2004), which is triggered by the diversity of student population in today's schools. Every time we pick up a newspaper, we read that schools are facing large populations of English language learners, some for the first time. And, as we've mentioned in previous chapters, the ELLs come with a variety of levels of language and literacy backgrounds.

Coaching is intended to support the systemic improvement of instruction and positive change efforts of schools (Kamil, 2003; National

Staff Development Council, 2001). The Standards for Middle and High School Literacy Coaches are meant to stiffen the resolve of education policymakers and schools that embrace coaching to do so mindfully, so this reform will not go the way of so many good intentions and produce minimal results (International Reading Association, 2006).

The culture that well-implemented coaching models engender is conducive to increased collective teacher and student learning. Effective coaching programs are designed to respond to particular needs suggested by data, allowing improvement efforts to target issues such as closing achievement gaps and supporting teachers across career stages, including meeting new certification requirements (Kamil, 2005).

Thus, coaching holds the potential to address inequities in opportunities for ELLs by providing differentiated, targeted supports to their teachers. A combined focus on content and the use of data encourages high quality instruction that reaches ELLs.

Evidence of increased student learning as a direct result of coaching is not yet well documented (Kamil, 2003). Although few empirical studies have been conducted on the effects of coaching teachers of ELLs, several of our studies have shown consistent positive results (Calderón, 1999; 2001). From these studies, we applied the best practices and refined these with current ones (Darling-Hammond & Brandsford, 2005; Kamil, 2005; Strickland, 2005).

One noticeable difference since our first study in 1984 is that the definition of coaching has evolved and is still evolving. It is becoming one of not only improving instruction but also helping teachers and administrators with a variety of tasks. In other words, the literacy coach coordinates and supports all services associated with literacy programs, which include coordinating professional development, curriculum distribution, student assessment, collection of data, and even writing proposals for funding—in addition to coaching teachers. For coaches in ELL contexts, the role becomes much more complex, with more tasks and a bigger role as teacher motivator and instructor. The IRA coaching standards outline key roles for coaches. We build upon these to address ELL issues.

The IRA Coaching Standards

The content area literacy standards apply to the demands literacy coaches face when assisting in a specific content area such as English language arts, mathematics, science, or social studies. Following is a summary of the four key competencies they have outlined:

Leadership Standards

STANDARD 1: SKILLFUL COLLABORATORS. Content area literacy coaches are skilled collaborators who function effectively in middle school and/or high school settings.

STANDARD 2: SKILLFUL JOB-EMBEDDED COACHES. Content area literacy coaches are skilled instructional coaches for secondary teachers in the core content areas of English language arts, mathematics, science, and social studies.

STANDARD 3: SKILLFUL EVALUATORS OF LITERACY NEEDS. Content area literacy coaches are skilled evaluators of literacy needs within various subject areas and are able to collaborate with secondary school leadership teams and teachers to interpret and use assessment data to inform instruction.

Content Area Standard

STANDARD 4: SKILLFUL INSTRUCTIONAL STRATEGISTS. Content area literacy coaches are accomplished middle and high school teachers who are skilled in developing and implementing instructional strategies for improving academic literacy in the specific content area.

The Standards Committee included recommendations on ELL instruction, such as the following:

1.3.1 Literacy coaches stay current with professional literature and the latest research on promising practices for adolescent literacy and adolescent ELL language development.

1.3.2 Literacy coaches routinely examine best practices and curriculum materials related to adolescent literacy for native and nonnative speakers of English.

1.3.5 Literacy coaches attend professional seminars, conventions, and other training in order to receive instruction on a core set of research-based literacy strategies and strategies for working with ELLs (those both literate and not literate in their native language) as well as to learn how to work effectively with adult learners.
   o Identify appropriate literacy scaffolding strategies that accommodate ELLs' different proficiency levels but move them toward grade-level literacy.

○ Focus on next steps, including how teachers might adjust instruction and instructional settings to meet a range of literacy needs of individual students, including ELLs, and to foster learning in the content area.

The Roles of a Literacy/ Content Coach in ELL Contexts

From our work with ExC-ELL schools, we have identified more specific roles for coaches of teachers with small or large numbers of ELLs. These are discussed in the sections that follow.

1. As coach for teachers with ELLs
   - Provide support for experienced teachers who may not have had training on new research-based reading through second language instruction
   - Provide support for teachers who need more help in integrating their content areas with reading through second-language instruction
   - Provide support for new teachers in the areas they need help
   - Provide motivation and support for all teachers for shifting from a mind-set that "ELLs are the ESL teacher's responsibility" to one of "ELLs are our responsibility"
   - Help create a cross-cultural climate to promote equity and enrichment.

2. As coordinator of professional development
   - Facilitate group and individual teacher development, by content areas or topics that cut across all disciplines
   - Observe, demonstrate, and confer with teachers focusing on ELL strategies
   - Schedule and effect collaboration and reflective dialog in Teachers' Learning Communities centering on ELL issues
   - Promote shared vision for policy and practice for quality ELL instruction

3. As coordinator of assessment
   - Identify appropriate assessments for ELLs
   - Assist in interpreting results: helps teachers determine individual ELLs' language and literacy levels
   - Conduct student surveys to gauge instructional appropriateness

- Work with teachers and administrators to conduct their own needs assessments
- Schedule/coordinate student assessments
- Conduct some student assessments

4. As curriculum and program developer or program sustainer
   - Work with others to select and evaluate curriculum materials best fitted to their ELL population
   - Coordinate selection committee activities
   - Provide resources/materials on a continuous basis
   - Motivate and help teachers to use the adopted program
   - Help teachers adapt program when necessary to reach all ELL students

5. As proposal writer
   - Work with others to determine funding possibilities that focus on ELLs
   - Write proposals with others to achieve program goals
   - Take charge of proposal follow-up

6. As researcher
   - Collect, organize, and interpret student and teacher data
   - Collaborate with researchers, program evaluators, and/or administrators to improve instruction
   - Interpret data for teachers to inform lesson and curriculum improvement

Juggling Multiple Roles

Coaching often focuses on broad strategies to the exclusion of differentiation and equity. For example, a literacy coach cannot simply help his or her teaching team learn a menu of "reading strategies," but must also attend to the unique learning needs of English language learners. Coaches and teachers can use disaggregated data on the language and learning needs of their students, and the professional cultures of their schools when they examine instructional practices. For example, a school with a large number of ELLs likely calls for instructional strategies that specifically address language acquisition in all classrooms and in tutoring or afterschool programs. A mainstream approach to reading or sheltering instruction would be insufficient to help teachers improve their practice to teach ELLs well and equitably.

Effective professional learning promotes positive cultural change. Coaches are effective liaisons between school practice and district initiatives. Effective coaches encourage collaborative, reflective practice. Most studies show that coaching leads to improvements in instructional capacity and thus a change in the culture of the school. For instance, with coaching, teachers apply their learning more deeply, frequently, and consistently than teachers working alone. Teachers improve their capacity to reflect and apply their learning not only to their work with students but also to their work with each other.

If the coaches are members of a districtwide team that seeks to improve the practice of all teachers, they serve as liaisons between teachers and administrators and between school and district, as well as serving as process facilitators and content experts. They are viewed as colleagues and allies rather than evaluators or administrators because they work to secure the central office supports required to sustain effective practice.

As coordinators of staff development, coaches identify the areas where teachers of ELLs are having difficulties in planning the lesson, parsing texts, selecting vocabulary to teach, identifying strategies for teaching vocabulary (7-step strategies, cognates and false cognates, roots and prefixes), and identifying metacognitive strategies to model and teach (before reading, during reading, or after reading) during writing or consolidation activities. When teachers are having difficulties with any instructional components, the coach should coordinate follow-up workshops, study sessions, and/or modeling of those strategies.

Coaching to Enhance the Quality of Instruction

Chapters 3 and 4 in this book give a précis of quality instructional elements for teachers of ELLs. Chapters 5–10 give examples of classroom instruction based on the ten-component lesson template. An observation protocol called the ExC-ELL Observation Protocol (EOP) was developed to go along with the classroom implementation. The EOP was developed, piloted, and validated through a grant from the Carnegie Corporation of New York to Johns Hopkins University. During that study, the ExC-ELL Observation Protocol was tested for validity and reliability (alpha .91) as a tool for the following:

- Collecting data on students' reading progress
- Classroom research
- Coaching by literacy coaches not familiar with ELL instruction
- Supervision by administrators
- Teacher self-reflection
- Peer coaching

For research purposes, the EOP provided a better understanding of the effects of the professional development intervention and how these effects vary according to factors such as (a) the quality of implementation and teacher support, (b) prior student performance, and (c) class size. For practical purposes, the EOP was designed for *literacy coaches, content curriculum specialists,* and *principals/administrators* to observe and coach teachers. Administrators and coaches were particularly interested in knowing how to observe and give feedback to teachers as they delivered their lessons integrating reading, writing, and vocabulary development along with their content.

The EOP can be used as a paper version or in a LogiTech version with software specifically developed for collecting important data during classroom observations. Student outcomes from the Gates MacGinitie pretests and posttests showed two or more grades growth for ExC-ELL students above their comparison groups when the EOP was used in the first pilot of the ExC-ELL study. Participating middle and high schools outperformed higher SES schools in the district for the first time and met AYP.

EOP Coaching Cycle

The coaching cycle is like any other cycle: (1) teacher and coach hold a preconference where the teacher states the objectives of the lesson, where the coach should focus the observation, determine the type of data most helpful to the teacher, and the desired goal(s) or outcomes; (2) the coach observes for those specific indicators and time frame as requested by the teacher and collects the necessary data on the EOP paper or LogiTech version; (3) the coach presents the data to the teacher at a postconference; (4) both teacher and coach analyze the data, discuss it, jointly agree on next steps or next things to work on, and schedule the next observation.

How to Use the EOP Indicators

Effective coaching programs need to use assessment indicators and systematic documentation of impact. The EOP indicators can be used to measure the changes in teachers' practice and assess the effectiveness of their work. For instance, a teacher can reflect on the items that were checked off a month before and compare to the current ones being checked off. Analyzing the differences between the two recordings with her coach will help her gauge the changes and adaptations already made and then compare these with the goals the teacher established at the beginning of the year.

The LogiTech version will also keep the teacher's and each student's data. For instance, the reading fluency data can be stored for individual students to keep running records on file. These records can then be downloaded from or onto a computer through the docking device.

Figure 10.1 The LogiTech Devices for the ExC-ELL Observation
          Protocol (EOP)

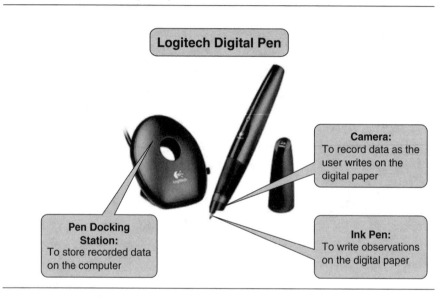

Each part of the protocol coincides with the lesson template. (See Figure 10.2 on page 133) The first page has spaces for drawing the context/layout of the classroom to indicate if students are sitting in teams or rows, if boys are sitting together and girls in separate teams, where the teacher moves in an out to monitor, etc. Observers use an X or a Y to indicate where boys or girls are sitting; they circle the student who responds most frequently, put tabs next to those whose behavior interrupts the class and how often, and so forth.

On the vocabulary page, the words written on the board can be recorded on the sheet, and the strategies being used to teach those words can be checked off. There is space for narrative in case some explanations or serendipitous event needs to be recorded. Each section provides these tools. The example of the Reading Compre-hension page (see Figure 10.3 on page 133) shows a teacher box and a box for recording the responses of selected students.

Figure 10.2 Example of the First Page of the EOP

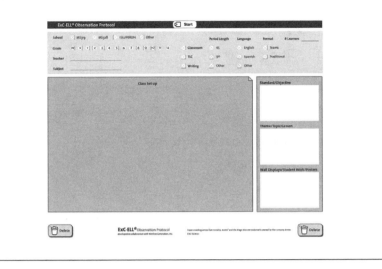

Figure 10.3 Example of a Reading Comprehension Page

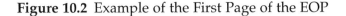

Once the data are recorded, these sheets can be used to give feedback to the teacher. The software generates six types of reports. Figure 10.3 shows one example. Presenting data through an observation protocol takes the burden off the coach because the data will speak for itself. The data are shown to the teacher, and the coach simply asks questions such as "What do you see here?" "How did you perceive your lesson?" "Do you want to ask me about any of this?"

Figure 10.4 The Data Collection and Reporting Options

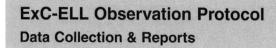

ExC-ELL Observation Protocol
Data Collection & Reports

- Logitech Digital Pen
  - ✓ a pen that records the data as it is written down on digital paper

- ExC-ELL Observation Protocol" Digital Form
  - ✓ 9-page digital paper form to note observations in the areas of Vocabulary, Oracy, Reading, Writing, Classroom Context and Assessment

- Reports
  - ✓ 6 types of reports can be created from the recorded data:
    - ○ Observation Summary Report
    - ○ Observation Detail Report
    - ○ Teacher Profile Summary Report
    - ○ Component Implementation Summary Report
    - ○ Vocabulary Usage Report
    - ○ Student Application Summary Report

After the data are presented, reflection for next steps takes place. Questions on vocabulary instruction for collegial discussions might be as follows for the vocabulary section:

- Are the students systematically interacting with the new words? Twelve exposures by teachers or twelve opportunities to produce the words in the first two days?
- Do students get to use the new words throughout the week?
- By the end of the week have they mastered for each word (1) pronunciation, (2) decoding, (3) meaning in context, (4) meaning in a different context, (5) spelling, and (6) use of the word in their own writing accurately and meaningfully?
- Do the vocabulary activities consist of time-consuming drawing of what a word means?
- Are students looking up the words in a dictionary? Or, is the teacher providing dictionary and student-friendly definitions?
- Do students make "pictionaries" where they write the word, draw a representation of its meaning, and never use them again?

> You can teach people nothing; you can only help them discover it within themselves.

It is important for coaches and teachers to go through formal training on how to use the observation protocol and how to coach, collect data, analyze data, give feedback, and use reflection questions. If training is not possible, the next best thing is to allocate time for coaches and teachers to work on coaching logistics and reach consensus on how to conduct their coaching routines. Coaching is a delicate endeavor. If the relationship between teacher and coach is not consensual or jointly agreed upon, it will not work.

Attributes of Effective Literacy/Content Coaches in ELL Contexts

- Is bilingual or in the process of learning another language
- Is flexible
- Is an effective teacher of ELLs and his or her subject area (language arts, math, science, social studies)
- Knows the research and best practices on reading/literacy development
- Knows the research and best practices on second-language literacy development
- Knows the national, state, and local policies for ELLs and all students
- Knows how to work with adults who are not used to teaching ELLs
- Knows how to give specific technical feedback
- Is highly motivated
- Is well organized
- Is highly collegial and likes to work in teams
- Is an effective leader, yet a team player
- Is a lifelong learner
- Is a problem solver
- Is discreet
- Is resilient
- Has a positive attitude and positive communication skills
- Is not a supervisor or an evaluator

Coaches themselves will need professional learning opportunities to refine their practice and align district initiatives and goals with ELL pedagogy. Professional learning for coaches integrates district reform strategies, content knowledge, and approaches to effective adult learning as well as continuous learning about literacy and language. As mentioned in Chapter 8, coaching is one element of a professional development system, not the only answer. Coaching is no silver bullet. It can sustain professional learning and act as a bridge between traditional school practice and enriched meaningful learning. However, for coaching to accomplish those ends, it must be explicitly linked to other professional development opportunities and broader components of systemic improvement, such as small learning communities or district-wide frameworks. If coaching or total dependency on literacy coaches is the only form of professional learning, it runs the risk of phasing itself out or leaving gaps in teacher learning.

Summary

- ✓ Change is difficult.
- ✓ If anyone has the courage to change, he/she will need support from peers, coaches, and supervisors.
- ✓ Empirically tested observation protocols for quality instruction for ELLs help create that positive change and climate in the schools.
- ✓ Empirically tested observation protocols help teachers reflect on their practice and seek feedback from trusted peers and experts.
- ✓ Coaches and supervisors need a lot of support and professional development also—particularly for observing quality instruction for ELLs in secondary schools.
- ✓ Coaching is a powerful tool, but a comprehensive staff development program that focuses on student outcomes must accompany it.
- ✓ Coaching is caring. It takes a lot of love to be a good coach.

References

Adams, M. J., Foorman, B. R., Lundberg, I., & Beeler, T. (1998). *Phonemic awareness in young children.* Baltimore, MD: Paul H. Brookes Publishing.

Anderson, R. (2002). Reforming science teaching: What research says about inquiry. *Journal of Science Teacher Education, 13*(1): 1–12.

Anderson, R. C., & Nagy, W. E. (1991). *Word meanings.* In R. Barr, M. L. Kamil, P. Mosenthal, & P.D. Pearson (Eds.), *Handbook of Reading Research: Vol. II* (pp. 690–724). Mahwah, NJ: Lawrence Erlbaum.

Armbruster, B. B., Anderson, T. H., & Ostertag, J. (1987). Improving content-area reading using instructional graphics. *Reading Research Quarterly, 26*(4), 393–416.

August, D. (2003). *Transitional programs for English language learners: Contextual factors and effective programming.* Baltimore, MD: Johns Hopkins University, Center for Research on the Education of Students Placed at Risk.

August, D., & Hakuta, K. (1997). *Improving schooling for language-minority children: A research agenda.* Washington, DC: National research council.

August, D., Calderón, M., & Carlo, M. (2001). Transfer of reading skills from Spanish to English: A study of young learners. *National Association for Bilingual Education Journal, 24*(4), 11–42.

August, D., Calderón, M., & Carlo, M. (2002). *Transfer of reading skills from Spanish to English: A study of young learners.* Report ED-98-CO-0071 to the Office of Bilingual Education and Minority Languages Affairs, U.S. Department of Education.

August, D., & Shanahan, T. (2006). *Developing literacy in second-language learners: Report of the National Literacy Panel on Language Minority Children and Youth.* Mahwah, NJ: Lawrence Erlbaum Associates.

Baker, C., & Prys Jones, S. (1998). *Encyclopedia of bilingualism and bilingual education.* Clevedon, England and Philadelphia, PA: Multilingual Matters.

Banks, J., Cochran-Smith, M., Moll, L., Richert, A., Zeichner, K., LePage, P., Darling-Hammond, L., & Duffy, H. (2005). Teaching diverse learners. In L. Darling-Hammond, & J. Bransford (Eds.), *Preparing teachers for a changing world: What teachers should learn and be able to do* (pp. 232–274). San Francisco: Jossey-Bass.

Barton, M. L., & Jordan, D. L. (2001). *Teaching reading in science.* Alexandria, VA: Association for Supervision and Curriculum Development.

Baumann, J. F. (1984). The effectiveness of a direct instruction paradigm for teaching main idea comprehension. *Reading Research Quarterly, 20*(1), 93–115.

Baumann, J. F., Edwards, E. C, Boland, E. M., Olejnik, S., & Kame'enui, E. J. (2003). Vocabulary tricks: Effects of instruction in morphology and context on fifth-grade students' ability to derive and infer word meanings. *American Educational Research Journal, 40*(2), 447–494.

Bear, D. Invernizzi, M., Templeton, S., & Johnston, F. (1996). *Words their way: Words study for phonics, vocabulary, and spelling.* Upper Saddle River, NJ: Pearson Education.

Beck, I. L., & McKeown, M. G. (1991). Conditions of vocabulary acquisition. In R. Barr, M. Kamil, P. Mosenthal, & P. D. Pearson (Eds.), *Handbook of reading research* (Vol. 2, pp. 787–814). White Plains, NY: Longman.

Beck, I. L., McKeown, M. G., Hamilton, R. L., & Kucan, L. (1997). *Questioning the author: An approach for enhancing student engagement with text.* Newark, DE: International Reading Association.

Beck, I. L., McKeown, M. G., & Kucan, L. (2002). *Bringing words to life.* New York: Guilford Press.

Beck, I. L., McKeown, M. G., & Kucan, L. (2005). Choosing words to teach. In E. H. Hiebert & M. L. Kamil (Eds.), *Teaching and learning vocabulary: Bringing research to practice* (pp. 207–222). Mahwah, NJ: Lawrence Erlbaum.

Berkowitz, S. (1986). Effects of instruction in text organization on sixth-grade students' memory for expository reading. *Reading Research Quarterly, 21*(2), 161–178.

Bialystok, E., & Hakuta, K. (1994). *In other words: The science and psychology of second-language acquisition.* New York: Basic Books.

Biancarosa, G., & Snow, C. E. (2004). *A vision for action and research in middle and high school literacy: A report from Carnegie Corporation of New York.* Washington, DC: Alliance for Excellent Education.

Biemiller, A. (1999). *Language and reading success. From reading research to practice: A series for teachers.* Neuton Upper Falls, MA: Brookline Books.

Biemiller, A., & Slonim, N. (2001). Estimating root word vocabulary growth in normative and advantaged populations: Evidence for a common sequence of vocabulary acquisition. *Journal of Educational Psychology, 93*(3), 498–520.

Blachowicz, C. L. Z., & Fisher, P. (2000). Vocabulary instruction. In M. L. Kamil, P. B. Mosenthal, P. D. Pearson, & R. Barr (Eds.), *Handbook of reading research* (Vol. 3, pp. 503–523). Mahwah, NJ: Lawrence Erlbaum.

Boscolo, P., & Mason, L. (2001). Writing to learn, writing to transfer. In P. Tynjala, L. Mason, & K. Lonka (Eds.), *Writing as a learning tool* (pp. 83–104). Dordrecht, The Netherlands: Kluwer Academic.

Bromley, K., Irwin-De Vitis, L., & Modlo, M. (1995). *Graphic organizers: Visual strategies for active learning.* New York: Scholastic Professional Books.

Brown, A. L., & Day, J. D. (1983). Macrorules for summarizing texts: The development of expertise. *Journal of Verbal Learning and Verbal Behavior, 22*(1), 1–14.

Calderón, M. (1994). Mentoring, peer support, and support systems for first-year minority/bilingual teachers. In R. A. DeVillar, C. J. Faltis, & J. P. Cummins (Eds.), *Cultural diversity in schools: From rhetoric to practice* (pp. 117–141). Albany, NY: State University of New York Press.

Calderón, M. (1998). *Staff Development in Multilingual Multicultural Schools. ERIC Digest.* New York: ERIC Clearinghouse on Urban Education.

Calderón, M. (1999). Teachers Learning Communities for cooperation in diverse settings. In M. Calderón & R. E. Slavin (Eds.), *Building community through cooperative learning* [Special issue]. *Theory into Practice, 38*(2), 94–99.

Calderón, M. (2000). *Teachers' learning communities (TLCs): Training manual.* El Paso, TX: CRESPAR.

Calderón, M. (2000). Teachers' Learning Communities for highly diverse classrooms. *National Association for Bilingual Education Journal, 24*(2), 33–34.

Calderón, M. (2001). Curricula and methodologies used to teach Spanish-speaking limited English proficient students to read English. In R. E. Slavin & M. Calderón (Eds.), *Effective programs for Latino students* (pp. 251–305). Mahwah, NJ: Lawrence Erlbaum.

Calderón, M. (2002). Trends in staff development for bilingual teachers. In L. Minaya-Rowe (Ed.), *Teacher training and effective pedagogy in the context of student diversity* (pp. 121–146). Greenwich, CT: Information Age.

Calderón, M. (submitted). Students' use of transfer skills and perceptions about transfer. *Journal of Education of Students Placed at Risk,* Baltimore, MD.

Calderón, M., August, D., & Minaya-Rowe, L. (2004). *ExC-ELL. Expediting comprehension for English-language learners.* New York: Carnegie Corporation of New York.

Calderón, M., August, D., Slavin, R. E., Duran, D. (in preparation). *The evaluation of a bilingual transition program for Success for All: A technical report.* Baltimore, MD: CRESPAR/Johns Hopkins University.

Calderón, M., August, D., Slavin, R. E., Duran, D., Madden, N., & Cheung, A. (2005). Bringing words to life in classrooms with English language learners. In E. H. Hiebert & M. L. Kamil (Eds.), *Teaching and learning vocabulary: Bringing research to practice* (pp. 115–136). Mahwah, NJ: Lawrence Erlbaum.

Calderón, M., Hertz-Lazarowitz, R., & Slavin, R. E. (1998). Effects of bilingual cooperative integrated reading and composition on students making the transition from Spanish to English reading. *The Elementary School Journal, 99*(2), 153–165.

Calderón, M., & Minaya-Rowe, L. (2003). *Designing and implementing two-way bilingual programs: A step-by-step guide for administrators, teachers, and Parents.* Thousand Oaks, CA: Corwin Press.

Calderón, M., Minaya-Rowe, L., & Carreón, A. (2006). *ExC-ELL. Expediting comprehension for English language learners: Teachers' manual.* Washington, DC: Margarita Calderón & Associates.

Calderón, M., Minaya-Rowe, L. & Duran, D. (2005). *Expediting comprehension to English language learners (ExC-ELL): Report to the Carnegie Foundation.* New York: Carnegie Corporation of New York.

Carlo, M. S., August, D., & Snow, C. E. (2005). Sustained vocabulary-learning strategy instruction for English language learners. In E. H. Hiebert & M. L. Kamil (Eds.), *Teaching and learning vocabulary: Bringing research to practice* (pp. 137–154). Mahwah, NJ: Lawrence Erlbaum.

Carlo, M., August, D., McLaughlin, B., Snow, C., Dressler, C., Lippman, D., Lively, T., & White, C. (2004). Closing the gap: Addressing the vocabulary needs of English language learners in bilingual and mainstream classrooms. *Reading Research Quarterly, 39,* 188–215.

Cayton, A., Perry, E. I., & Winkler, A. M. (1995). *America. Pathways to the present.* Needham, MA: Prentice Hall.

Center for Applied Linguistics. (2005). *Guiding principles for dual-language education.* Washington, DC: Author.

Center for Applied Linguistics. (2006). *Directory of two-way bilingual immersion programs.* Retrieved from the World Wide Web July 18, 2006, at www .cal.org/twi/directory/tables.hmt/#table2

Chall, J. S. (1996). American reading achievement: Should we worry? *Research in the Teaching of English, 30,* 303–310.

Chamot, A. U., & O'Malley, J. M. (1994). *The CALLA handbook: Implementing the cognitive academic language learning approach.* New York: Addison-Wesley.

Chamot, A. U., & O'Malley, J. M. (1996). The cognitive academic language learning approach: A model for linguistically diverse classrooms. *Elementary School Journal, 96*(3), 259–273.

Clair, N., & Adger, C. T. (1999). *Professional development for teachers in culturally diverse schools.* Retrieved from the World Wide Web December 10, 2003, at www.cal.org/ericcll/

Connecticut State of Department of Education. (2004). *English language learner (ELL) frameworks.* Hartford, CT: Author.

Coolidge-Stoltz, E., Graff-Haight, D., Jenner, J., Cronkite, D., Holtzclaw, F., & Cronin Jones, L. (2002). *Life science.* Upper Saddle River, NJ: Prentice Hall.

Crawford, J. (1999). *Bilingual education: History, politics, theory, and practice* (4th ed.). Los Angeles: Bilingual Educational Services.

Crowther, S. (1998). Secrets of staff development support. *Educational Leadership, 55*(5), 75–76.

Cummins, J. (1984). *Bilingualism and special education: Issues in assessment and pedagogy.* London: Multilingual Matters.

Cunningham, A. E., & Stanovich, K. E. (1998). What reading does for the mind. *American Educator,* Spring-Summer, 8–17.

Dansereau, D. F. (1988). Cooperative learning strategies. In C. E. Weinstein, E. T. Goetz, & P. A. Alexander (Eds.), *Learning and study strategies: Issues in assessment, instruction, and evaluation* (pp. 103–120). Orlando, FL: Academic Press.

Darling-Hammond, L., (1998). Teacher learning that supports student learning. *Educational Leadership, 55*(5), 6–11.

Darling-Hammond, L., & McLaughlin, M. W. (1995). Policies that support professional development in an era of reform. *Phi Delta Kappan, 76*(8), 597–604.

Darling-Hammond, L., & Sykes, G. (2003) Wanted: A national teacher supply policy for education: The right way to meet the "highly qualified teacher" challenge. *Educational Policy Analysis Archives, 11* (33). Retrieved from the World Wide Web April 13, 2005, at http://epaa.asu.edu/epaa/ v11n33/

Darling-Hammond, L., & Bransford, J. (Eds.). (2005). *Preparing teachers for a changing world: What teachers should learn and be able to do.* San Francisco: Jossey-Bass.

Davey, B., & McBride, S. (1986). Effects of question generating training on reading comprehension. *Journal of Educational Psychology, 78*(4), 256–262.

Davis, E. A., & Krajcik, J. S. (2005). Designing educative curriculum materials to promote teacher learning. *Educational Researcher 34*(3), 3–14.

Delgado Gaitán, C. (2004). *Involving Latino families in schools: Raising student achievement through home-school partnerships.* Thousand Oaks, CA: Corwin Press.

Dewitz, P., Carr, E., & Patberg, J. (1987). Effects of interference training on comprehension and comprehension monitoring. *Reading Research Quarterly, 22,* 99–121.

DiSpezio, M., Lisowski, M., Skoog, G., Linner-Luebe, M., & Sparks, B. (1999). *Science Insights: Exploring living things.* Menlo Park, CA: Addison Wesley.

Dobson, K., Holman, J., Roberts, M. (1996). *Science spectrum: A physical approach.* Austin, TX: Holt, Rinehart and Winston.

Doty, J. K., Cameron, G. N., & Barton, M. L. (2003). *Teaching reading in the social studies.* Aurora, CO: Mid-Continent Research for Education & Learning.

Dowhower, S. L. (1987). Effects of repeated reading on second-grade transitional readers' fluency and comprehension. *Reading Research Quarterly, 22,* 389–406.

Echevarria, J., & Graves, A. (1998). *Sheltered content instruction: Teaching students with diverse abilities.* Boston: Allyn & Bacon.

Echevarria, J., & Graves, M. (2005). Curriculum adaptations. In P. A. Richard-Amato & M. A. Snow (Eds.). *Academic success for English language learners: Strategies for K-12 mainstream teachers* (pp. 224–247). White Plains, NY: Longman.

Echevarria, J., Vogt, M. E., & Short, D. J. (2000). *Making content comprehensible for English language learners: The SIOP model.* Boston: Allyn & Bacon.

Ehri, L. C. (1998). Grapheme-phoneme knowledge is essential for learning to read words in English. In L. Metsala & L.C. Erhi (Eds.), *Word recognition in beginning literacy* (pp. 3–40). Mahwah, NJ: Lawrence Erlbaum.

Eldredge, J. L. (1990). Increasing the performance of poor readers in the third grade with a group-assisted strategy. *Journal of Educational Research, 84,* 69–77.

Fantuzzo, J. W., Polite, K., & Grayson, N. (1990). An evaluation of reciprocal peer tutoring across elementary school settings. *Journal of School Psychology, 28,* 309–323.

Fillmore, L. W. & Snow, C. E. (2002) What teachers need to know about language. In C. T. Adger, C. E. Snow, & D. Christian (Eds.), *What teachers need to know about language.* Washington, DC: Center for Applied Linguistics and Delta Systems.

Fitzgerald, J. (1995). English-as-a-second-language reading instruction in the United States: A research review. *Journal of Reading Behavior, 27*(2), 115–152.

Flores, B., Cousin, P. T., & Díaz, E. (1998). Transforming deficit myths about learning, language, and culture. In M. F. Opitz (Ed.), *Literacy instruction for culturally and linguistically diverse students* (pp. 27–38). Newark, DE: International Reading Association.

Flower, L., & Hayes, J. (1980). The dynamics of composing: Making plans and juggling constraints. In L. Gregg and E. Steinberg (Eds.), *Cognitive processes in writing.* Hillsdale, NJ: Lawrence Erlbaum.

Foorman, B. R., & Mehta, P. (2002, November). *Definitions of fluency: Conceptual and methodological challenges.* PowerPoint presentation at A Focus on Fluency Forum, San Francisco, CA. Available at http://www.prel.org/programs/rel/fluency/Foorman.ppt

Fountas, I. C., & Pinnell, G. S. (2001). *Guiding readers and writers, grades 3–6: Teaching comprehension, genre, and content literacy.* Portsmouth, NH: Heinemann.

Freeman, Y. S., & Freeman, D. E. (2002). *Closing the achievement gap: How to reach limited-formal-schooling and long-term English learners.* Portsmouth, NH: Heinemann.

Freeman, Y. S., Freeman, D. E., & Mercuri, S. (2003). Helping middle and high school age English language learners achieve academic success. *NABE Journal of Research and Practice 1*(1), 110–122.

Garcia, E. (1999). *Student cultural diversity: Understanding and meeting the challenge* (2nd ed.). Boston: Houghton Mifflin.

García, G. E. (2000). Bilingual children's reading. In M. L. Kamil, P. B. Mosenthal, P. D. Pearson, & R. Barr (Eds.), *Handbook of reading research* (Vol. 3, pp. 813–834). Mahwah, NJ: Lawrence Erlbaum.

Genesee, F. (1999). *Program alternatives for linguistically diverse students.* Santa Cruz, CA: Center for Research in Education, Diversity & Excellence.

Genesee, F., Lindholm-Leary, K., Saunders, W., & Christian, D. (2005). English language learners in US schools: An overview of research findings. *Journal of Education for Students Placed At Risk, 10*(4), 363–385.

Gersten, R. (1996). Literacy instruction for language minority students: The transition years. *The Elementary School Journal,* 96(3), 228–244.

Goldenberg, C. (1992/1993). Instructional conversations: Promoting comprehension through discussion. *The Reading Teacher, 46,* 316–326.

Gonzalez, J. M. & Darling-Hammond, L. (1997). *New concepts for new challenges: Professional development for teachers of immigrant youth.* McHenry, IL: Delta Systems and CAL.

Gottlieb, M. (1999). Assessing ESOL adolescents: Balancing accessibility to learn with accountability for learning. In C. J. Faltis & P. Wolfe (Eds.), *So much to say: Adolescents, bilingualism and ESL in the secondary school* (pp. 176–201). New York: Teachers College Press.

Gottlieb, M. (2006). *Assessing English language learners. Bridges from language proficiency to academic achievement.* Thousand Oaks, CA: Corwin Press.

Graham, R. L., & Gill, D. L. T. (1972). *Dove.* New York: Harper & Row.

Graves, M. F., Cooke, C. L., & Laberge, M. J. (1983). Effects of previewing difficult short stories on low ability junior high students' comprehension, recall, and attitudes. *Reading Research Quarterly, 18*(3), 262–276.

Grosso de León, A. (2002). *The urban high school's challenge: Ensuring literacy for every child.* New York: Carnegie Corporation of New York.

Guskey, T. (1998). Follow-up is key, but it's often forgotten. *Journal of Staff Development, 19*(2), 7–8.

Guskey, T. (2000). *Evaluating professional development.* Thousand Oaks, CA: Corwin Press.

Hansche, L. (1998). *Handbook for the development of performance standards: Meeting the requirements of Title I.* Washington, DC: U.S. Department of Education, Office of Educational Research and Improvement.

Hansen, J., & Pearson, P. D. (1983). An instructional study: Improving the inferential comprehension of fourth grade good and poor readers. *Journal of Educational Psychology, 75*(6), 821–829.

Hirsch, E. D., Hart, B., Risley, T. R., & Beck, I. L. (Eds.). (2003). The fourth grade plunge: The cause. The cure [Special issue]. *American Educator.* Washington, DC: American Federation of Teachers.

Holt, Rinehart, and Winston. (2003). *World history: The human journey.* Austin, TX: Author.

Howard, E. R., Sugarman, J., & Christian, D. (2003). *Two-way immersion education: What we know and what we need to know.* Baltimore: Johns Hopkins University, CRESPAR.

Howard, E., Sugarman, J., Perdomo, M., & Adger, C. (2005). *The two-way immersion toolkit.* Washington, DC: Center for Applied Linguistics.

Idol, L. (1987). Group story mapping: A comprehension strategy for both skilled and unskilled readers. *Journal of Learning Disabilities, 20*(4), 196–205.

Idol, L., & Croll, V. J. (1987). Story-mapping training as a means of improving reading comprehension. *Learning Disability Quarterly, 10*(3), 214–229.

International Reading Association. (2001). *Second-language literacy instruction. A position statement of the International Reading Association.* Newark, DE: Author.

International Reading Association. (2006, June/July). Hot topic: NCLB. *Reading Today, 23*(6), 20.

International Reading Association. (2006). *Standards for middle and high school literacy coaches.* Newark, DE: Author.

Ivey, G. & Fisher, G. (2005, October). Learning from what doesn't work. *Educational Leadership, 63*(2), 8–14.

Joyce, B., & Showers, B. (1988). *Student achievement through staff development.* New York: Longman.

Joyce, B., & Showers, B. (2002). *Student achievement through staff development* (3rd ed.). Alexandria, VA: Association for Supervision and Curriculum Development.

Juel, C. (1988). Learning to read and write: A longitudinal study of 54 children from first through fourth grades. *Journal of Educational Psychology, 80,* 437–447.

Kamil, M. (2003). *Adolescents and literacy.* Washington, DC: Alliance for Excellent Education.

Kamil, M. L. (2005, June). *Review of key findings of NCLB legislation and research.* PowerPoint presentation, PREL Focus on Professional Development in Early Reading Forum, Honolulu.

Kamil, M. L., & Hiebert, E. H. (2005). Teaching and learning vocabulary: Perspectives and persistent issues. In E. H. Hiebert & M. L. Kamil (Eds.). *Teaching and learning vocabulary: Bringing research to practice* (pp. 1–23). Mahwah, NJ: Lawrence Erlbaum.

Kindler, A. L. (2002). *Survey of the states' limited English proficient students and available educational programs and services: 2000–2001 summary report.* Washington, DC: National Clearinghouse for English Language Acquisition and Language Instruction Educational Programs.

King, A. (1994). Guiding knowledge construction in the classroom: Effects of teaching children how to question and explain. *American Educational Research Journal, 31*(2), 338–368.

King, M., Fagan, B., Bratt, T., & Baer, R. (1987). ESL and social studies integration. In J. Crandall (Ed.), *ESL through content area instruction: Mathematics, science, social studies* (pp. 89–119). Arlington, VA: Center for Applied Linguistics.

Klingner, J. K., & Vaughn, S. (1998). Using collaborative strategic reading. *Teaching Exceptional Children, 30*(6), 32–37.

Koskinen, P. S., & Blum, I. H. (1986). Paired repeated reading: A classroom strategy for developing fluent reading. *The Reading Teacher, 40,* 70–75.

Krashen, S. (1982). *Principles and practice in second language acquisition.* Oxford, UK: Pergamon.

Krashen, S. D. (1981). Bilingual education and second language acquisition theory. In California State Department of Education (Ed.), *Schooling and language minority students: A theoretical framework* (pp. 51–82). Los Angeles, CA: Evaluation, Dissemination, and Assessment Center.

Kreeft Peyton, J. (2005). *Using the ESL program standards to evaluate and improve adult ESL programs.* Retrieved July 10, 2005, from the Center for Adult English Language Acquisition (CAELA) at the Center for Applied Linguistics Web site, www.cal.org

Kuhn, M., & Stahl, S. (2000). *Fluency: A review of developmental and remedial practices* (Report No.2–0008). Ann Arbor, MI: Center for the Improvement of Early Reading Achievement.

LaBerge, D., & Samuels, S. J. (1974). Toward a theory of automatic information processing in reading. *Cognitive Psychology, 6,* 293–323.

Langan, J., & Johnson, B. (2004). *English essentials: What everyone needs to know about grammar, punctuation, and usage.* West Berlin, NJ: Townsend Press, Inc.

Langer, J. A. (1981). From theory to practice: A pre-reading plan. *Journal of Reading, 25,* 152–156.

Laughlin, C. W., & Thompson, M. (1999). *Physical science.* New York: Glencoe/McGraw-Hill.

Lazarowitz, R., & Karsenty. G. (1990). Cooperative learning and students' academic achievement, process skills, learning environment, and self esteem in tenth grade biology classrooms. In S. Sharan (Ed.), *Cooperative learning: Theory and research* (pp. 123–149). New York: Praeger.

Learning First Alliance. (2000). *Every child reading: A professional development guide.* Baltimore, MD: Association for Supervision and Curriculum Development.

Lieberman, A. (1995). Practices that support teacher development. *Phi Delta Kappan 76*(8), 591–596.

Leibowitz, A. H. (1980). *The bilingual education act: A legislative analysis.* Washington, DC: National Clearinghouse for Bilingual Education.

Lenski, S. D., Wham, M. A., & Johns, J. L. (1999). *Reading and learning strategies for middle & high school students.* Dubuque, IA: Kendall/Hunt.

Leos, K. (2006, June). Introductory remarks at the SIFE Share Fair. New York City Department of Education, Office of English Language Learners, New York City.

Lindholm-Leary, K. J. (2001). *Dual language education.* Clevedon, England and Buffalo, NY: Multilingual Matters.

Linquanti, R. (1999). *Fostering Academic Success for English Language Learners: What Do We Know?* Retrieved July 15, 2005, from the WestEd Web site, www.wested.org/cs/we/view/rs/514

Lyons, C. A., & Pinnell, G. S. (2001). *Systems for change in literacy education. A guide to professional development.* Portsmouth, NH: Heinemann.

Malone, L. D., & Mastropieri, M. A. (1992). Reading comprehension instruction: Summarization and self-monitoring training for students with learning disabilities. *Exceptional Children, 58,* 270–279.

Mandel Morrow, L. (2003). Make professional development a priority. President's message in *Reading Today* 21 (1) 6–7. Newark, DE: International Reading Association.

Marzano, R. J., Pickering, D. J., & Pollock, J. E. (2001). *Classroom instruction that works: Research-based strategies for increasing academic achievement.* Alexandria, VA: Association for Supervision and Curriculum Development.

Maton, A., LaHart, D., Hopkins, J., Warner, M. Q., Johnson, S., & Wright, J. (1995). *Exploring physical science.* Englewood Cliffs, NJ: Prentice Hall.

McDonnell, H., Miller, J. E., & Hogan, R. J. (1989). *Traditions in literature: America reads.* Sunnyvale, CA: Scott Foresman.

McEwan, E. K. (2001) *Raising reading achievement in middle and high schools.* Thousand Oaks, CA: Corwin Press.

McKenna, M. C., & Robinson, R. D. (1990). Content literacy: A definition and implications. *Journal of Reading, 34,* 184–186.

Meloth, M. S., & Deering, P. D. (1992). The effects of two cooperative conditions on peer group discussions, reading comprehension, and metacognition. *Contemporary Educational Psychology, 17,* 175–193.

Meloth, M. S., & Deering, P. D. (1994). Task talk and task awareness under different cooperative learning conditions. *American Educational Research Journal, 31*(1), 138–165.

Menken, K., & Antúnez, B. (2001). *An overview of the preparation and certification of teachers working with low English proficiency students.* Washington, DC: National Clearinghouse for Bilingual Education.

Menon, S., & Hiebert, E. H. (2003, April). *A comparison of first graders' reading acquisition with little books and literature anthologies.* Paper presented at the annual meeting of the American Educational Research Association, Chicago, IL.

Moir, E., & Bloom, G. (2003). Fostering leadership through mentoring. *Educational Leadership, 60*(8), 58–61.

Nagy, W. (2005). Why vocabulary instruction needs to be long-term and comprehensive. In E. H. Hiebert & M. L. Kamil (Eds.), *Teaching and learning vocabulary: Bringing research to practice* (pp. 27–44). Mahwah, NJ: Lawrence Erlbaum.

Nagy, W. E., & Anderson, R. C. (1984). How many words are there in printed school English? *Reading Research Quarterly, 19*(3), 304–330.

Nagy, W. E., Garcia, G. E., Durgunoglu, A. Y., & Hancin-Bhatt, B. (1993). Spanish-English bilingual students' use of cognates in English reading. *Journal of Reading Behavior, 25,* 241–259.

Nagy, W. E., & Herman, P. A. (1987). Breadth and depth of vocabulary knowledge: Implications for acquisition and instruction. In M. G. McKeown &

M. E. Curtis (Eds.), *The nature of vocabulary acquisition* (pp. 19–35). Hillsdale, NJ: Erlbaum.

National Center for Education Statistics (2001). *Teacher preparation and professional development: 2000.* Washington, DC: Author.

National Center for Education Statistics. (2002). *The condition of education, 2002.* Washington U.S. Department of Education.

National Center for Education Statistics. (2003). *The condition of education, 2003.* Washington U.S. Department of Education.

National Center for Education Statistics. (2006). *The condition of education, 2006.* Washington U.S. Department of Education.

National Council for the Social Studies. (1997). *A sampler of curriculum standards for social studies: Expectations of excellence.* Upper Saddle River, NJ: Prentice Hall.

National Council of Teachers of English. (2000). *English teachers pass resolution on high-stakes testing and the rights of test takers.* Urbana, IL: Author.

National Council of Teachers of English & International Reading Association. (1996). *Standards for English Language Arts.* Retrieved from the World Wide Web April 10, 2004, at www.ncte.org/standards

National Council of Teachers of Mathematics. (1989). *Curriculum and evaluation standards for school mathematics.* Reston, VA: Author.

National Council of Teachers of Mathematics. (2000). *Principles and standards for school mathematics.* Reston, VA: Author.

National Institute of Child Health and Human Development. (2000). *Teaching children to read: An evidence-based assessment of the scientific research literature on reading and its implications for reading instruction.* (NIH Publication No. 00–4754). Washington, DC: U.S. Government Printing Office.

National Literacy Panel on Language Minority Children and Youth. (in preparation). *Report on teaching reading to language minority children and youth.* Washington, DC: National Institute of Child Health and Human Development, National Institutes of Health, and Institute on Educational Science, U.S. Department of Education.

National Panel on Literacy for Adolescent English Language Learners. (2006). *Double the work: Academic literacy for adolescent English language learners.* New York: Carnegie Corporation of New York.

National Reading Panel. (2000). *Teaching children to read: An evidence-based assessment of the scientific research literature on reading and its implications for reading instruction.* Rockville, MD: National Institute of Child Health and Human Development.

National Research Council. (1996). *National science education standards.* Washington, DC: National Academy Press.

National Staff Development Council. (2001). *National Staff Development Council's standards for staff development, revised.* Oxford, OH: Author.

Northwest Regional Education Laboratory. (2004). *English language learner (ELL) programs at the secondary level in relation to student performance.* Portland, OR: Author

Ogbu, J., & Matute-Bianchi, M. E. (1986). Understanding sociocultural factors: Knowledge, identity, and school adjustment. In California State Department of Education (Ed.), *Beyond language: Social and cultural factors in schooling language minority students* (pp. 73–142). Los Angeles:

California State University, Evaluation, Dissemination, and Assessment Center.

Ogbu, J. U. (1992). Understanding cultural diversity and learning. *Educational Researcher, 21*(8), 5–14.

Olshavsky, J. E. (1976–1977). Reading as problem solving: An investigation of strategies. *Reading Research Quarterly, 12*(4), 654–764.

Optiz, M. F. (Ed.). (1998). *Literacy instruction for culturally and linguistically diverse students: A collection of articles and commentaries.* Newark, DE: International Reading Association.

Osborn, J., Lehr, F., & Heibert, E. H. (2003). *A focus on fluency.* Monograph published by Pacific Resources for Education and Learning. Retrieved from http://www.prel.org/programs/rel/rel.asp

Ovando, C. J., & Collier, V. P. (1998). *Bilingual and ESL classrooms: Teaching in multicultural contexts* (2nd ed.). Boston: McGraw-Hill.

Ovando, C. J., Collier, V. P., & Combs, M. C. (2003). *Bilingual and ESL classrooms. Teaching in multicultural contexts* (3rd ed.). Boston: McGraw Hill.

Pacific Resources for Education and Learning. (2002). *Readings on fluency for "A focus on fluency forum."* Honolulu, HI: Author.

Padrón, Y. N. (1992). The effect of strategy instruction on bilingual students' cognitive strategy use in reading. *Bilingual Research Journal, 16*(3&4), 35–52.

Padrón, Y. N., & Waxman, H. C. (1988). The effect of ESL students' perceptions of their cognitive reading strategies on reading achievement. *TESOL Quarterly, 22,* 146–150.

Palincsar, A. S., & Brown, A. L. (1984). Reciprocal teaching of comprehension fostering and comprehension monitoring activities. *Cognition and Instruction, 2,* 117–175.

Palincsar, A. S., & Brown, A. L. (1986). Interactive teaching to promote independent learning from text. *The Reading Teacher, 39*(8), 771–777.

Paris, S. C., & Paris, A. H. (2001). Classroom applications of research on self-regulated learning. *Educational Psychologist, 36*(2), 89–101.

Pressley, M. (1998). *Reading instruction that works: The case for balanced teaching.* New York: Guilford.

Pressley, M. (2003). Psychology of literacy and literacy instruction. In W. M. Reynolds & G. E. Miller (Vol. Eds.), *Handbook of Psychology,* Vol. 7 (pp. 333–356). Hoboken, NJ: Wiley.

Pressley, M., & Afflerbach, P. (1995). *Verbal protocols of reading: The nature of constructively responsible reading.* Hillsdale, NJ: Lawrence Erlbaum.

Pressley, M., Levin, J.R., & Delaney, H. (1982). The mnemonic keyword method. *Review of Educational Research, 52,* 61–92.

Pressley, M., & Woloshyn, V. (1995). *Cognitive strategy instruction that really improves children's academic performance* (2nd ed.). Cambridge, MA: Brookline Books.

Pugalee, D. K. (2002). Beyond numbers: Communicating in math class. *ENC Focus, 9*(2), 29–32.

RAND Reading Study Group. (2002). *Reading for understanding: Toward and research and development program in reading comprehension.* Retrieved July 7, 2005, from the RAND Web site at www.rand.org/publications .html

Rasinski, T. V. (2000). Speed does matter in reading. *The Reading Teacher, 54,* 146–150.

Rasinski, T. V. (2004). *Assessing reading fluency.* Honolulu, HI: Pacific Resources for Education and Learning.

Robertson, L., Davidson, N., & Dees, R. L. (1994). Cooperative learning to support thinking, reasoning, and communicating in mathematics. In S. Sharan (Ed.), *Handbook of cooperative learning methods* (pp. 245–266). Westport, CT: Praeger.

Rosenshine, B., & Meister, C. (1994, April). *A comparison of results with standardized tests and experimenter-developed comprehension tests when teaching cognitive strategies.* Paper presented at the annual meeting of the American Educational Research Association, New Orleans.

Samuels, S. J. (2002). Reading fluency: Its development and assessment. In Pacific Resources for Education and Learning (Ed.), *Readings on fluency for "A focus on fluency forum."* Honolulu, HI: PREL.

Saunders, W., & Goldenberg, C. (1999). Effects of instructional conversations and literature logs on limited and fluent English proficient students' story comprehension and thematic understanding. *Elementary School Journal, 99*(4), 277–301.

Saunders, W., O'Brien, G., Lennon, D., & McLean, J. (1998). Making the transition to English literacy successful: Effective strategies for studying literature with transition students. In R. Gersten & R. Jiménez (Eds.), *Promoting learning for culturally and linguistically diverse students* (pp. 99–132). New York: Wadsworth.

Saunders, W. M. (2001). Improving literacy achievement for English learners in transitional bilingual programs. In R. E. Slavin & M. Calderón (Eds.), *Effective programs for Latino students* (pp. 171–206). Mahwah, NJ: Lawrence Erlbaum.

Schifini, A. (2000). *Second language learning at its best: The stages of language acquisition.* Carmel, CA: Hampton Brown Publishers.

Schunk, D. H., & Cox, P. D. (1986). Strategy training and attributional feedback with learning disabled students. *Journal of Educational Psychology, 78,* 201–209.

Schunk, D. H., & Swartz, C. W. (1993). Goals and progressive feedback: Effects on self-efficacy and writing achievement. *Contemporary Educational Psychology, 18,* 337–354.

Scott, J. A. (2005). Creating opportunities to acquire new word meanings from text. In E. H. Hiebert & M. L. Kamil (Eds.), *Teaching and learning vocabulary: Bringing research to practice* (pp. 69–91). Mahwah, NJ: Lawrence Erlbaum.

Shanahan, T. (2002, November). *A sin of the second kind: The neglect of fluency instruction and what we can do about it.* PowerPoint presentation at A Focus on Fluency Forum, San Francisco, CA. Available at http://www.prel .org/programs/rel/fluency/Shanahan.ppt

Shanker, J. L., & Ekwall, E. E. (1998). *Locating and correcting reading difficulties* (7th ed.). Upper Saddle River, NJ: Prentice Hall.

Short, D. (1994). Expanding middle school horizons: Integrating language, culture, and social studies. *TESOL Quarterly, 28,* 581–608.

Short, D. (1999). Integrating language and content for effective sheltered instruction programs. In C. Faltis & P. Wolfe (Eds.), *So much to say:*

Adolescents, bilingualism, and ESL in the secondary school (pp. 105–137). New York: Teachers College Press.

Short, D. J., & Boyson, B. A. (2003). *Establishing and effective newcomer program.* Retrieved August 7, 2005, from the Center for Applied Linguistics Web site at www.cal.org/resources/digest/0312short.html

Short, E. J., & Ryan, E. B. (1984). Metacognitive differences between skilled and less skilled readers: Remediating deficits through story grammar and attribution training. *Journal of Educational Psychology, 76,* 225–235.

Slavin, R. E., & Calderón, M. (Eds.) (2001). *Effective programs for Latino students.* Mahwah, NJ: Lawrence Erlbaum.

Slavin, R. E., & Cheung, A. (2004). How do English language learners learn to read? *Educational Leadership, 61*(6), 52–57.

Slavin, R. E., & Cheung, A. (in press). *Effective reading approaches for English language learners: Language of instruction and replicable programs.* A technical report. Baltimore, MD: CRESPAR, Johns Hopkins University.

Slavin, R. E., & Madden, N. A. (1999). Effects of bilingual and English as second language adaptations of Success for All on the reading achievement of students acquiring English. *Journal of Education for Students Placed at Risk, 4*(4), 393–416.

Slavin, R. E., & Madden, N. A. (2001). *One million children: Success for all.* Thousand Oaks, CA: Corwin Press.

Snow, C. (2002). *Reading for understanding: Toward a research and development program in reading comprehension.* Santa Monica: RAND Corporation.

Snow, C., Burns, S., & Griffin, P. (1998). *Preventing reading difficulties in young children.* Washington, DC: National Academy Press.

Spanier, B. (1992). Encountering the biological sciences: Ideology, language, and learning. In A. Herrington & C. Moran (Eds.), *Writing, teaching, and learning in the disciplines* (pp. 193–212). New York: Modern Language Association.

Sparks, D., & Hirsh, S. (1997). *A new vision for staff development.* Alexandria, VA: Association for Supervision and Curriculum Development.

Spellings, M. (2005, December). Remarks at fourth annual "Celebrate Our Rising Stars Summit: From Essential Elements to Effective Practice," Washington, DC. Retrieved May 20, 2006, from http://ncela .gwu.edu

Spellings, M. (2006, April). Remarks at No Child Left Behind summit: The path to 2014 in Philadelphia. Retrieved May 20, 2006, from http://ncela .gwu.edu

Stahl, S. A. (1999). *Vocabulary development. From Reading Research to Practice: A Series for Teachers.* Cambridge: MA: Brookline Books.

Stahl, S. A. (2003). How words are learned incrementally over multiple exposures. In E. D. Hirsch, B. Hart, T. R. Risley, & I. L. Beck (Eds.), *The fourth grade plunge: The cause. The cure* (Special issue). Washington, DC: American Federation of Teachers.

Stahl, S. A. (2005). Four problems with teaching word meanings: And what to do to make vocabulary and integral part of instruction. In E. H. Hiebert & M. L. Kamil (Eds.), *Teaching and learning vocabulary: Bringing research to practice* (pp. 95–114). Mahwah, NJ: Lawrence Erlbaum Associates, Inc.

Stevens, R. J., Slavin, R. E., & Farnish, A. M. (1991). The effects of cooperative learning and direct instruction in reading comprehension strategies on main idea identification. *Journal of Educational Psychology, 83*(1), 8–16.

Stoddart, T., Pinales, A., Latzke, M., & Canaday, D. (2002). Integrating inquiry science and language development for English language learners. *Journal of Research in Science Teaching, 39*(8), 664–687.

Strickland, D. S. (2005, June). *New direction in professional development: The literacy coach.* PowerPoint presentation, PREL Focus on Professional Development in Early Reading Forum, Honolulu.

Stuckey, S., & Salvucci, L. K. (2000). *Call to freedom.* Austin, TX: Holt, Rinehart and Winston.

Suro, R., & Passel, J. S. (2003). *The rise of the second generation: Changing patterns in Hispanic population growth.* Retrieved from the World Wide Web November 1, 2003, at www.pewhispanic.org

Taylor, B. M., & Beach, R. W. (1984). Effects of text structure instruction on middle-grade students' comprehension and production of expository text. *Reading Research Quarterly, 19*(2), 147–161.

Taylor, B. M., Pearson, P. D., Peterson, D. S., & Rodriguez, M. C. (2003). Reading growth in high-poverty classrooms: The influence of teacher practices that encourage cognitive engagement in literacy learning. *Elementary School Journal, 104,* 3–28.

Teachers of English to Speakers of Other Languages. (2006). *ESL standards for pre-K-12 students.* Alexandria, VA: Author.

Tharp, R. G., Estrada, P., Dalton, S. S., & Yamauchi, L. A. (2000). *Teaching transformed: Achieving excellence, fairness, inclusion, and harmony.* Boulder, CO: Westview Press.

Tharp, R. G., & Yamauchi, L. A. (1994). Effective instructional conversation in Native American classrooms. *Center for Research on Education, Diversity and Excellence,* Paper EPR10.

Thompson, D. R., & Rubenstein, R. N. (2000). Learning mathematics vocabulary: Potential pitfalls and instructional strategies. *Mathematics Teacher 93(7),* 568–574.

Tierney, R. J., & Pearson, P. D. (1994). Learning to learn from text: A framework for improving classroom practice. In R. B. Ruddell & H. Singer (Eds.), *Theoretical models and processes of reading* (4th ed.) (pp. 496–513). Newark, DE: International Reading Association.

Tierney, R. J., & Readence, J. E. (2000). *Reading strategies and practices: A compendium* (5th ed.). Boston: Allyn and Bacon.

Torgesen, J. K., Rashotte, C. A., Alexander, A. W., Alexander, J., & McFee, K. (2002, November). *The challenge of fluent reading for older children with reading difficulties.* PowerPoint presentation at A Focus on Fluency Forum, San Francisco, CA. Available at http://www.prel.org/programs/rel/fluency/Torgesen.ppt

United States Census Bureau. (2000). *Statistical abstract of the United States 2000.* Washington, DC: Author.

United States Census Bureau. (2001). *Current population survey, March 2000.* Washington, DC: Author.

United States Department of Education. (2003). *Nation's report card: Reading 2002.* Retrieved January 5, 2004, from the National Center for Education Statistics Web site at nces.ed.gov/pubsearch/pubsinfo.asp?pubid=2003521

United States Department of Education. (2005). *Biennial evaluation report to Congress on the implementation of Title III, Part A of the ESEA.* Retrieved August 5, 2005, from the National Clearinghouse for English Language Acquisition Web site at http://www.ncela.gwu.edu/oela/biennia105

Usiskin, Z. (1996). Mathematics as a language. In P. C. Elliott & M. J. Kenney (Eds.) *Communication in Mathematics, K–12 and Beyond, 1996 Yearbook of the National Council of Teachers of Mathematics* (pp. 66–75; 143–231). Reston, VA: NCTM.

Valdéz, G. (1996). *Con respeto.* New York: Teachers College Press.

Valdés, G. (2001). *Learning and not learning English: Latino students in American schools.* New York: Teachers College Press.

Verhoeven, L., & Snow, C. (Eds.). (2001). *Literacy and motivation. Reading engagement in individuals and groups.* Mahwah, NJ: Lawrence Erlbaum.

Wagonner, D. (1999). Who are secondary newcomer and linguistically different youth? In C. J. Faltis & P. Wolfe (Eds.), *So much to say: Adolescents, bilingualism & ESL in the secondary school* (pp. 13–41). New York: Teachers College Press.

Walqui, A. (2005). Who are our students? In P. A. Richard-Amato & M. A. Snow (Eds.), *Academic success for English language learners: Strategies for K–12 mainstream teachers* (pp. 7–21). White Plains, NY: Pearson Education.

Walsh, K. (2003). The lost opportunity to build knowledge that propels comprehension. In E. D. Hirsch, B. Hart, T. R. Risley, & I. L Beck (Vol. Eds.), The fourth grade plunge: The cause. The cure (Special issue). *American Educator* (pp. 24–27). Washington, DC: American Federation of Teachers.

Wenglinsky, H. (2002). *How teaching matters: Bringing the classroom back into discussions of teacher quality.* Princeton, NJ: Educational Testing Service.

Wilbraham, A. C., Staley, D. D., Simpson, C. J., & Matta, M. S. (1993). *Chemistry.* Menlo Park, CA: Addison-Wesley.

Zimmerman, B. J., Bonner, S., & Kovach, R. (1996). *Developing self-regulated learners: Beyond achievement to self-efficacy.* Washington, DC: American Psychological Association.

Index

CORWIN PRESS

The Corwin Press logo—a raven striding across an open book—represents the union of courage and learning. Corwin Press is committed to improving education for all learners by publishing books and other professional development resources for those serving the field of PreK–12 education. By providing practical, hands-on materials, Corwin Press continues to carry out the promise of its motto: **"Helping Educators Do Their Work Better."**